GETTING STARTED IN

CRYPTO

21 Day Beginner Guide

By Lisa N Edwards

Trading Books

Become a Millionaire in One Year

BeLikeLisa Trading Journal Pink/Blue/Grey

Fiction Novels

Can't Fight Fate
Chasing Butterflies
Seed of the Sunflower

GETTING STARTED IN CRYPTO

21 Day Beginner Guide

Lisa N Edwards

GETTING STARTED IN CRYPTO
21 Day Beginner Guide
by Lisa N Edwards

ISBN: 978-0-6486443-4-7 PRINT

Published by Visual Media Group
Docklands Melbourne Australia 3008
vmg@visualmediagroup.com.au
www.visualmediagroup.com.au

Cataloguing-in-Publication data is available from the National Library of Australia

The Only Way to Make Money

Is Make Your Own!

Lisa N Edwards

Success in Crypto Starts with the Right Mindset

- ***Lisa N. Edwards***

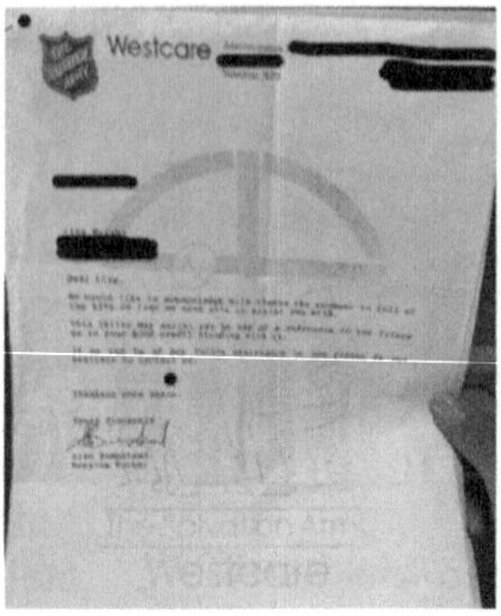
Westcare [redacted]

[redacted]

[redacted]

Cryptocurrency is more than just numbers on a screen, it's about building habits, discipline, and a long-term vision. Your mindset will make or break you in this space. Markets are volatile, and emotions like fear and greed can lead to poor decisions.

Understanding your risk tolerance and staying calm during market swings is what separates winners from those who panic-sell.

For Lisa N Edwards, trading has been a lifeline, not just a skill. She learned to trade at just 16 while working a part-time job at KFC. A regular customer, a junior analyst, saw her potential, especially after she placed among the top in an Australian national math competition and decided to mentor her. He armed her with the skills to turn small amounts of income into much larger sums, a skillset that has served her well throughout her life.

Lisa's ability to trade helped her navigate one of the toughest times of her life, moving to Melbourne with her baby daughter nearly 30 years ago. Couch-surfing with friends, she found herself in financial uncertainty. A chance encounter led her to a Salvation Army loan program, but instead of relying solely on assistance, she leveraged her trading knowledge to secure her own rental property, cover living expenses, and eventually repay the Salvos in full.

As a mother of five and, at times, a single mother, her trading skills have been invaluable. Trading wasn't just about making money—it was about survival, resilience, and creating opportunities.

Now, as the Managing Partner of Visual Media Group, Lisa has built a crypto empire designed to make the industry less toxic, more female-friendly, and accessible to all regardless of age or gender. She's a seasoned trader with 30 years of experience in stocks and commodities and a decade in cryptocurrency trading.

A master of Elliott Wave theory, she's also developed her own approach to market analysis, what she affectionately calls Lisanachi—a fusion of Fibonacci, support and resistance, volume profiles, and key trading indicators.

Lisa has ranked among the top traders on TradingView, managed private and public crypto funds, and led top-tier trading groups. But her expertise extends far beyond finance, she's an award-winning screenwriter, actress, and novelist with a deep understanding of human psychology, both in storytelling and trading. She knows what moves the market and how to help others level up.

Her journey proves that success isn't just about market knowledge, it's about mindset, resilience, and the drive to push forward. The most successful investors visualise their wealth before it exists. Whether it's setting clear goals, journaling progress, or creating a vision board, having a long-term perspective keeps you grounded.

Lisa's story is a testament to what's possible when you combine strategy with an unstoppable mindset. Now, let's dive into the fundamentals of cryptocurrency and set you up for success

Visual Media Group Brands
https://visualmediagroup.com.au/

Getting Started In Crypto
https://gettingstartedincrypto.com/

Thousand to Millions
https://thousandtomillions.com/

Be Like Lisa
https://belikelisa.com/

Personal Links
https://linktr.ee/LisaNEdwards

Money is only a tool.

It will take you wherever you wish, but it will not replace you as the driver.

Ayn Rand

DISCLAIMER

The following disclaimer applies to the book titled *21-Day Crypto Mastery – Your Guide to Getting Started In Crypto* (hereinafter referred to as "the Book"). By reading and utilising the information provided in this Book, you acknowledge and agree to the terms set forth in this disclaimer.

1. **Informational Purposes Only**: The Book is intended to provide general information on emotional regulation, psychology, and mindset for traders. It is not a substitute for professional mental health support, therapy, or financial advice.

2. **No Psychological or Medical Advice**: While the Book discusses emotional resilience and psychological principles, it is not intended to diagnose, treat, or replace professional mental health services. If you are experiencing mental health challenges, it is strongly advised that you seek support from a qualified psychologist, therapist, or medical professional.

3. **Individual Results May Vary**: The concepts and techniques outlined in the Book are based on research and the author's personal experience. Results may differ for each individual, and the author makes no guarantees regarding improvements in emotional regulation, trading performance, or overall well-being.

4. **Personal Responsibility**: The information in the Book is intended for educational and self-improvement purposes. Readers are solely responsible for their actions, decisions, and any outcomes resulting from the application of the ideas presented. The author and publisher disclaim any liability for consequences arising from the use of this material.

5. **No Guarantees of Success**: Emotional regulation is a complex and personal process. While the Book aims to support traders in managing their emotions effectively, it does not promise specific outcomes in trading performance or financial success.

6. **External References**: The Book may mention external resources, research, or psychological principles for informational purposes. The author and publisher do not endorse or guarantee the accuracy or effectiveness of any third-party sources. Readers should conduct their own research and consult professionals as needed.

7. **Intellectual Property**: All intellectual property rights related to the Book, including but not limited to copyrights and trademarks, belong to the author and publisher. No part of the Book may be reproduced, distributed, or transmitted in any form without prior written permission.

By reading and utilising the information in the Book, you acknowledge that you have read, understood, and agreed to the terms and conditions set forth in this disclaimer.

Published Date:4 March 2025 Author: Lisa N Edwards
Publisher: Visual Media Group - Books P/L

"I trained 4 years to run only 9 seconds.

There are people who do not see results in 2 months, give up and leave. Sometimes failure is sought by oneself."

Usain Bolt

Acknowledgements

*A huge thank you to **Josh Taylor**—the behind-the-scenes awesomeness who takes care of all the things I can't stand doing. Your effort never goes unnoticed, and I appreciate you more than words can say. Love you!*

THANK YOU!

"Every life is a story. Thank you for being part of mine."

Lisa

CONTENTS

PREFACE

INTRODUCTION

Daily Habits Checklist

- 10 minutes of meditation or journaling.
- 30–40 minutes of exercise or movement.
- 1 hour for personal growth or contribution projects.
- 1 connection-focused action (call, message, or quality time).
- 1 fun or adventurous activity (small or big).

Before We Start - The Crypto Basics

- Success in Crypto Starts with Daily Habits
- Your Mindset Will Make or Break You in Crypto
- Risk vs. Reward – Finding Your Comfort Zone
- There's no right or wrong answer here—it's about knowing yourself.
- Visualise Your Future Wealth
- Before We Dive In

Day 0: Understanding Cryptocurrency and Blockchain

- What is Cryptocurrency?
- How is Cryptocurrency Different from Traditional Money?
- How Blockchain Technology Works
- What is Blockchain?
- How Transactions Work on a Blockchain
- Types of Blockchains
- Why Decentralization Matters
- How Does Decentralization Benefit You?
- Real-World Example: Bitcoin in Venezuela

WEEK 1: Foundational Wealth Psychology

Day 1: Introduction: Build a Wealth Mindset

- Day 1 begins!
- Emphasise the importance of mindset in wealth creation.
- Share a powerful quote (e.g., *"Your mindset is your greatest asset."*).

Day 2: The Psychology of Money

- Discuss emotional biases like fear and greed.
- Introduce strategies to stay rational in trading.
- Action tip: Start a "trading journal" to log decisions and emotions.

Day 3: Overcoming the Scarcity Mindset

- Explain how scarcity thinking limits risk-taking and growth.
- Share steps to cultivate an abundance mindset.

Day 4: Patience: The Wealth Builder's Superpower

- Why patience is critical in crypto and investing.
- Highlight the dangers of impulsive trading.
- Tip: Use tools like limit orders to remove emotion from trading.

Day 5: Your Relationship with Risk

- Break down risk tolerance vs. risk capacity.
- Teach readers how to create a risk management plan.

Day 6: Setting SMART Financial Goals

- Guide readers in defining Specific, Measurable, Achievable, Relevant, and Time-bound goals.
- Share an example goal (e.g., *"Accumulate 1 BTC by 2025."*).

Day 7: Visualisation: See Your Wealth Before It Exists

- Teach visualisation techniques to solidify financial goals.
- Include an exercise for creating a vision board or wealth journal.

WEEK 2: Crypto Trading Strategies

Day 8: The Basics of Technical Analysis

- Explain candlesticks, support/resistance, and trends.
- Include a chart example to analyse.

Day 9: Fundamental Analysis for Crypto

- Teach how to evaluate a project: team, utility, and tokenomics.
- Share tools like CoinMarketCap and Glassnode.

Day 10: Risk Management in Trading

- Cover position sizing, stop-loss orders, and risk/reward ratios.
- Action tip: Risk no more than 2% of your capital per trade.

Day 11: Mastering Market Cycles

- Explain bull and bear markets in crypto.
- Include historical examples (e.g., Bitcoin's 2017 bull run).

Day 12: The Power of Dollar-Cost Averaging (DCA)

- Teach how to build positions over time with DCA.
- Share a real-world example of DCA with Bitcoin.

Day 13: How to Spot Trends and Stay Ahead

- Discuss moving averages, RSI, and MACD as trend indicators.
- Tip: Combine technical with news events for better timing.

Day 14: Common Crypto Trading Mistakes

- List top errors: overtrading, ignoring fees, chasing pumps.
- Action tip: Pause and reassess if tempted by FOMO.

WEEK 3: Advanced Strategies and Wealth Habits

Day 15: Leveraging DeFi and Staking

- Teach how to earn passive income through staking and DeFi platforms.
- Mention popular protocols like AAVE, Lido, and PancakeSwap.

Day 16: Tax Strategies for Crypto Investors

- Explain basic tax rules and record-keeping for crypto gains.
- GettingStartedinCrypto.com.

Day 17: Diversification: More Than Just Bitcoin

- Share the importance of diversifying within and outside crypto.
- Include examples of altcoins, stablecoins, and traditional assets.

Day 18: Preparing for the Next Bull Run

- Share how to identify early indicators of market recovery.
- Encourage readers to position themselves for future gains.

Day 19: Mental Resilience for Traders

- Discuss the importance of managing stress and maintaining discipline.
- Tip: Use mindfulness techniques to reduce anxiety during volatile markets.

Day 20: Networking and Community Involvement

- Highlight the value of joining crypto communities (e.g., Discords, Twitter spaces).
- Suggest following influential traders and educators.

Day 21: Closing: Your Wealth-Building Blueprint

- Summarise key lessons from the newsletter series.
- Include a free checklist or resource (e.g., a trading strategy template).
- Call to action: Encourage readers to revisit lessons and start applying them today.

Preface

Cryptocurrency is no longer just a buzzword, it's a financial revolution reshaping how we think about money, investments, and financial freedom.

Yet, for many, crypto remains a mystery filled with technical jargon, volatility, and uncertainty. The goal of this book is to cut through the noise and provide you with a structured, step-by-step approach to mastering crypto in just 21 days.

I have spent years navigating the highs and lows of the crypto markets, learning valuable lessons along the way. I've seen fortunes made overnight, and I've seen people lose everything due to lack of knowledge or poor security practices. This book is designed to ensure you are informed, prepared, and confident as you embark on your own crypto journey.

Unlike other guides that overwhelm you with information, this book follows a habit-forming 21-day approach, because knowledge alone isn't enough. Real success comes from applying what you learn consistently. Over the next three weeks, you'll gain practical insights, hands-on strategies, and a clear path to integrating crypto into your financial future.

Whether you're completely new to the space or looking to refine your skills, this book will help you:

Understand the core principles of cryptocurrency and blockchain technology.

Navigate exchanges, wallets, and security best practices with ease.

Build a smart, risk-managed approach to investing and trading.

Explore advanced topics like DeFi, NFTs, staking, and long-term wealth-building strategies.

Develop the mindset and discipline needed to thrive in this fast-paced industry.

This book isn't just about theory, it's about action. Each day builds upon the last, giving you a solid foundation to confidently participate in the crypto space by the end of the 21 days. By following the steps outlined here, you'll avoid common pitfalls, seize opportunities, and set yourself up for long-term success in the world of cryptocurrency.

I'm excited for you to embark on this journey. Let's build this habit together, one day at a time.

The future of finance is here.

Are you ready to master it?

Introduction

Why 21 Days?

They say it takes 21 days to build a habit, and when it comes to cryptocurrency, consistency is key. The crypto space can be overwhelming, with its constantly evolving landscape, new technologies, and volatile markets. But by dedicating just a few minutes each day to learning and applying new skills, you can develop the confidence and expertise needed to make informed decisions in this digital financial revolution.

This eBook is designed to help you integrate cryptocurrency into your daily routine, whether you're completely new to the space or looking to refine your investment strategies. Over the next 21 days, you'll receive structured, easy-to-follow lessons that break down complex concepts into actionable steps.

- By the end of this journey, you will:
- Understand the core principles of blockchain and cryptocurrency.
- Know how to securely buy, store, and trade digital assets.
- Recognise key market trends and avoid common pitfalls.

- Explore advanced topics like DeFi, NFTs, and staking.
- Develop long-term strategies for investing and wealth-building.

The goal isn't just to provide information, it's to help you build a lasting habit of staying informed, making strategic moves, and gaining financial independence through cryptocurrency. Let's dive in and make the next 21 days a transformative experience for your financial future!

Before We Start - The Crypto Basics

Welcome to your 21-Day Crypto Mastery journey!

If you've ever felt overwhelmed by the world of cryptocurrency, you're not alone. All those terms—Bitcoin, blockchain, DeFi, trading strategies—can feel like a foreign language at first. But don't worry, you're in the right place.

Think of this as your crypto boot camp—a simple, structured guide to help you not just understand the world of crypto but thrive in it. By the time you finish, you'll have a solid grasp on how to navigate the market, avoid common mistakes, and build wealth with confidence.

Before we dive in, let's talk about something crucial: your mindset.

Success in Crypto Starts with Daily Habits

You might think crypto success is all about technical analysis, trading, and market trends—and while those are important, the real secret? Daily habits.

Great investors, traders, and entrepreneurs all have one thing in common: they follow a routine that keeps them sharp, focused, and resilient.

Here's a simple daily checklist to keep you on track:

- Take 10 minutes to clear your mind—through meditation, journaling, or just reflecting on the day.
- Move your body for 30–40 minutes—whether it's a walk, workout, or stretching.
- Spend 1 hour on personal growth—reading, listening to a podcast, or working on a passion project.
- Connect with someone—call a friend, network in the crypto space, or engage with a community.
- Do something fun or adventurous—crypto isn't just about numbers; balance is key!

These may seem unrelated to investing but trust me—discipline in your daily life leads to discipline in your financial decisions.

Now, let's talk about why mindset matters.

Your Mindset Will Make or Break You in Crypto

Crypto is one of the most exciting, yet emotionally challenging markets. Prices can skyrocket overnight—but they can crash just as fast. If you don't have the right mindset, it's easy to panic sell, chase pumps, or make impulsive decisions that can cost you money.

Think of it this way: your emotions are your biggest opponent in investing.

When prices drop, fear takes over—"Should I sell before it crashes further?"
When prices surge, greed kicks in—"I need to buy more before it's too late!"

This is where most people fail. They let their emotions control their actions instead of following a strategy.

So, how do you avoid this?

- Start a trading journal. Write down every decision you make, along with how you're feeling at the time. Over time, you'll start recognising patterns in your behaviour—and you'll learn how to stay calm and logical instead of reactive.
- Adopt an abundance mindset. Many people think, "I missed my chance to invest in Bitcoin early, so I've missed out on crypto." But that's simply not true. There are always new opportunities—if you're paying attention. Instead of worrying about what you *missed*, focus on where the market is heading next.
- Play the long game. Wealth isn't built overnight. The most successful investors in crypto aren't the ones constantly chasing hype—they're the ones who patiently accumulate and hold strong positions over time.

Risk vs. Reward – Finding Your Comfort Zone

Let's talk about risk.

Crypto investing isn't about gambling—it's about taking smart, calculated risks.

The first step? Understanding your own risk tolerance.

Ask yourself:

- How much am I willing to lose without affecting my financial stability?
- Can I handle seeing my investment drop 30% without panicking?
- Do I want slow, steady growth or am I comfortable with high volatility?

There's no right or wrong answer here—it's about knowing yourself.

A few golden rules:
✓ Never invest more than you can afford to lose.
✓ Diversify your investments. Don't put everything into one coin—spread your risk.
✓ Use stop-loss orders to automatically sell if prices drop too much.

By setting clear risk-management rules, you'll stay in control—no matter what the market throws at you.

Set Clear, Achievable Financial Goals

Here's something most people overlook when they start investing setting clear goals.

If you don't have a target, you're just guessing—and guessing leads to bad decisions.

Instead of saying "I want to make money in crypto," be specific:

- "I want to accumulate 1 Bitcoin by 2025 by investing $200 per month."
- "I want to generate $500/month in passive income through staking by next year."

Clear goals help you:

- Stay focused. When you know what you're working toward, it's easier to avoid distractions.
- Make better decisions. Every action should align with your long-term goal.
- Track progress. You'll know if you're on the right path—or if adjustments are needed.

Visualise Your Future Wealth

This might sound a little "out there," but visualisation is a powerful tool.

The most successful investors see their success before it happens.

Here's how you can do it:

- Create a vision board. Find images of financial freedom, travel, investments, and anything that represents success for you.
- Write in a wealth journal. Describe your financial goals in detail.
- Use affirmations. Repeat phrases like "I am a smart and disciplined investor" daily.

By training your brain to believe in your future success, you'll naturally start making better decisions.

Before We Dive In

So, before we even get into crypto strategies, charts, and trading, let's recap:

✓ Develop daily success habits. Consistency is key.

✓ Train your mindset. Fear and greed are your biggest enemies—control them.

✓ Manage risk wisely. Have a plan before you invest.

✓ Set clear, achievable goals. This keeps you on track.

✓ Visualise your wealth. If you can see it, you can achieve it.

With these foundational principles in place, you're ready to start your crypto journey the right way—not just as another hype-chaser, but as a smart, strategic investor.

Now, let's get started with how to securely store your crypto and avoid common pitfalls.

The Rule of 100

If you spend 100 hours a year in any discipline,

(which is only ~18 minutes a day)

you'll be better than 95% of the world in that discipline.

Consistency is everything.

"Money is multiplied in practical value depending on the number of W's you control in your life:

What you do. When you do it, and with Whom you do it."

Tim Ferris

Day 0

Understanding Cryptocurrency and Blockchain

Welcome to the first day of your 21-Day Crypto Mastery journey! Today, we'll break down the fundamentals of cryptocurrency and blockchain technology in a way that's easy to understand, whether you're new to the space or looking to reinforce your knowledge.

By the end of this chapter, you'll have a clear understanding of:

- What cryptocurrency is and how it works.
- The basics of blockchain technology.
- Why decentralization matters and how it empowers financial freedom.

Let's Get Started in Crypto!

What is Cryptocurrency?

A New Kind of Money

Cryptocurrency is digital money that is secured by cryptography, making it nearly impossible to counterfeit or manipulate. Unlike traditional currencies (such as the US Dollar or Euro), cryptocurrencies are decentralized, meaning they are not controlled by a government or financial institution.

The most well-known cryptocurrency is **Bitcoin (BTC)**, but thousands of other cryptocurrencies (also called "altcoins") exist, each with unique features and purposes.

Key Features of Cryptocurrency:

- **Decentralized:** No central authority (like a bank) controls it.
- **Digital & Borderless:** Transactions happen over the internet, anywhere in the world.
- **Secure:** Uses cryptographic encryption to prevent fraud.
- **Transparent:** Every transaction is recorded on a public ledger.
- **Fast & Low-Cost:** No intermediaries, which means fewer fees and faster transfers.

How is Cryptocurrency Different from Traditional Money?

Feature	Traditional Money (Fiat)	Cryptocurrency
Control	Centralized (Governments & Banks)	Decentralized (No single authority)
Physical Form	Paper, Coins	100% Digital
Supply	Unlimited (Governments can print more)	Limited (Bitcoin has a max supply of 21 million)
Security	Susceptible to inflation & counterfeiting	Secured by blockchain technology
Transaction Speed	Can take days (especially cross-border)	Instant to a few minutes
Fees	Bank & exchange fees can be high	Lower fees due to no intermediaries

Unlike fiat currencies that can lose value due to inflation, many cryptocurrencies have fixed supplies, making them more resistant to devaluation.

How Blockchain Technology Works

Now that you understand cryptocurrency, let's discuss blockchain, the technology that makes crypto secure and decentralized.

What is Blockchain?

A blockchain is a digital ledger that records transactions in a transparent and secure way. Instead of being stored on a single server (like a bank's database), blockchain transactions are recorded across thousands of computers (nodes) worldwide.

Imagine a Google Spreadsheet that anyone can view, but no one can change old entries.

That's blockchain in simple terms—it is:

- Public – Anyone can see transactions.
- Immutable – Once a transaction is added, it cannot be changed.
- Secure – Every transaction is verified before being recorded.

How Transactions Work on a Blockchain

1. A transaction is initiated. (Example: Alice sends 1 BTC to Bob.)
2. The transaction is broadcast to a network of computers.
3. Miners or validators verify the transaction. (Solving cryptographic puzzles to confirm legitimacy.)
4. Once verified, the transaction is added to a "block."
5. The block is linked to the previous block, forming a chain.
6. The transaction is permanently recorded and cannot be altered.

Analogy: Imagine a digital notebook where every page (block) records transactions, and each page is linked to the previous one in an unbreakable chain.

This technology ensures that no single entity can manipulate the system—making cryptocurrency one of the most secure financial systems ever created.

Types of Blockchains

There are different types of blockchains, depending on how open or restricted they are:

1. Public Blockchains – Open to everyone, anyone can participate (e.g., Bitcoin, Ethereum).
2. Private Blockchains – Restricted access, controlled by an organisation (e.g., used by banks & enterprises).
3. Hybrid Blockchains – A mix of both public and private (used for specific business applications).

For cryptocurrencies like Bitcoin and Ethereum, a public blockchain is used, meaning no single entity controls the network, ensuring true decentralization.

Smart Contracts – The Backbone of DeFi & NFTs

Smart contracts are self-executing agreements written in code and stored on the blockchain. They remove the need for middlemen, allowing trustless transactions between parties.

Benefits of Smart Contracts Automation – No need for human intervention (e.g., automatic loan repayments in DeFi).

Transparency – Anyone can verify the contract's logic on-chain.

Security – Reduces fraud risks since transactions are irreversible.

Real-World Examples:

- DeFi – Uniswap uses smart contracts for automated trading.
- NFTs – Ownership of digital art and assets (e.g., COINRUNNERS).
- Insurance – Payouts triggered automatically in parametric insurance policies.

Why Decentralization Matters

One of the biggest advantages of cryptocurrency is that it operates in a decentralized system. This means no government, corporation, or central bank has control over the network.

How Does Decentralization Benefit You?

- **Financial Freedom:** No government can freeze or seize your funds.
- **No Middlemen:** Transactions occur directly between people, reducing fees.
- **Censorship-Resistant:** No one can block a transaction from happening.
- **More Secure:** Hackers can't attack a single point of failure (since the network is spread across thousands of nodes).

Real-World Example: Bitcoin in Venezuela

In countries like Venezuela, where hyperinflation has destroyed local currency value, Bitcoin has become a lifeline. People use BTC to store wealth, buy goods, and send money internationally without government restrictions.

This is why cryptocurrency isn't just about making money—it's about financial empowerment.

Congratulations! You now have a strong understanding of cryptocurrency and blockchain technology. Today, we covered:

- What cryptocurrency is and why it's different from traditional money.
- How blockchain technology ensures security and transparency.
- The power of decentralization and its real-world benefits.

Crypto Exchanges – Choosing the Right One

Centralised vs Decentralised Exchanges (CEX vs DEX)

When buying and trading crypto, you need an exchange. There are two main types:

- Centralised Exchanges (CEX) – Platforms like Binance, Coinbase, and Kraken where transactions are managed by a third party.
- Decentralised Exchanges (DEX) – Platforms like Uniswap and PancakeSwap where users trade peer-to-peer with no middleman.

Pros & Cons of Each Exchange Type

◆ Centralised Exchanges (CEX)

✓ Easier for beginners – User-friendly interfaces and customer support.
✓ Liquidity – Higher trading volume means faster transactions and better prices.
✓ Fiat On-Ramps – Buy crypto directly with credit cards or bank transfers.

Risks:

- Custodial risk – You don't control your private keys.
- Hacks & Freezing – Exchanges have been hacked, and governments can freeze funds.
- Regulatory Dependence – Some exchanges operate in grey areas without full licenses.

Choosing a Secure CEX:

If you use a centralised exchange, make sure it has:

- Merkle Tree Proof-of-Reserves – Ensures the exchange actually holds user funds.
- Regulatory Licensing – Look for compliance with frameworks like MiCA (Markets in Crypto-Assets Regulation) in the EU.
- Insurance & Security Measures – Some exchanges provide fund insurance and strong security protocols.

◆ **Decentralised Exchanges (DEX)**

- Privacy & Control – You control your own private keys and funds.
- No Third-Party Risks – No central authority can freeze your assets.
- Access to Early-Stage Crypto Projects – Many new tokens launch on DEXs first.

Risks:

- More complex – Requires knowledge of blockchain transactions and smart contracts.

- Smart contract risks – Bugs or exploits in the contract can lead to lost funds.

- Liquidity issues – Lower volume can mean higher price slippage on trades.

Safety Tips for Using Exchanges

- Never keep large amounts on an exchange – Always transfer long-term holdings to a secure wallet.
- Enable Two-Factor Authentication (2FA) – Adds an extra layer of security to logins.
- Use strong passwords – Avoid common passwords and enable password managers.
- Be cautious of phishing scams – Always verify you're on the official exchange website.

By understanding the differences between CEX and DEX and following best security practices, you can trade confidently while keeping your funds safe.

How to Safely Store Your Crypto – Understanding Wallets

If you want to succeed in crypto, security is everything. One of the biggest mistakes beginners make is leaving their assets on an exchange, exposing them to potential hacks, frozen accounts, or even exchange collapses (think Mt. Gox or FTX). The best way to protect your funds is by using a crypto wallet.

Advanced Security Practices in Crypto

Protecting Your Crypto from Scams & Hacks

- Phishing Scams – Fake emails and websites trick you into revealing private keys.
- Rug Pulls – Fraudulent projects that disappear after taking investors' money.
- SIM Swap Attacks – Hackers steal your phone number to bypass 2FA.

Best Security Practices:

✓ Never share your private keys or recovery phrase.

✓ Use a hardware wallet for long-term storage.

✓ Always verify website URLs before entering credentials.

✓ Keep backup copies of your recovery phrase in secure locations.

What is a Crypto Wallet?

A crypto wallet is a tool that allows you to store, send, and receive cryptocurrency securely. Unlike traditional wallets, which hold physical cash, crypto wallets store **private keys**—these are essentially the passwords that give you access to your funds on the blockchain.

Types of Crypto Wallets

There are two main categories:

Hot Wallets (Connected to the Internet)

Hot wallets are convenient and easy to use, but they come with a higher risk since they are online and vulnerable to hacking.

Types of Hot Wallets:

- Web Wallets – Built into exchanges like Binance or Coinbase (not recommended for long-term storage).
- Mobile Wallets – Apps like Trust Wallet or MetaMask allow you to manage your funds on the go.
- Desktop Wallets – Software like Exodus or Electrum runs on your computer for added control.

Best for: Active traders, small amounts of crypto, and quick transactions.

Risks: If your device is compromised, so is your wallet. Always enable two-factor authentication (2FA) and use strong passwords.

Cold Wallets (Offline & Secure)

Cold wallets are the gold standard for security since they keep your private keys offline, safe from hackers.

Types of Cold Wallets:

- Hardware Wallets – Devices like Ledger Nano X and Trezor securely store your private keys offline.
- Paper Wallets – A printed QR code of your private key stored safely (highly secure but easy to lose).

Best for: Long-term storage, large holdings, and investors who prioritise security.

Risks: If you lose your hardware wallet AND recovery phrase, you may lose access to your funds forever. Always store your backup phrase securely!

How to Choose the Right Wallet

The best wallet depends on your needs:

- If you trade frequently, a hot wallet is more convenient.
- If you're a long-term investor, a hardware wallet is a must.
- For DeFi, NFTs, and Web3, consider MetaMask or Trust Wallet for easy integration.

Security Best Practices

- NEVER share your private keys or recovery phrase. Legitimate support teams will NEVER ask for them.
- Use a strong password and enable 2FA.
- Beware of phishing scams – always check website URLs before logging in.
- Keep a secure backup of your recovery phrase in multiple safe locations.
- For large amounts, use cold storage and only move funds to a hot wallet when needed.

Crypto gives you full control over your money, but with that control comes responsibility. Exchanges can be hacked. Wallets can be lost. But if you follow these security measures, your crypto will always be in your hands.

This foundational knowledge will help you confidently navigate the crypto world as you progress through this 21-day journey.

WEEK 1

Foundational Wealth Psychology

DAY 1

Building the Foundation of Crypto Success

Reprogram Your Mindset for Wealth

Welcome to your first step toward financial mastery! Before we dive into the technical side of cryptocurrency, let's get one thing straight—success in crypto (or anything in life) starts with your mindset.

You can learn all the strategies, market trends, and trading techniques in the world, but if your mindset is working against you, you'll struggle to make real progress. Wealth isn't just about what you know—it's about how you think, act, and approach opportunities.

So, let's start by reprogramming your mindset for wealth, success, and financial freedom.

Success in Crypto Starts with Daily Habits

You don't just wake up one day as a successful trader or investor—it's the small, consistent actions you take every day that get you there.

Here's a daily checklist to keep you on track:

- 10 minutes of meditation or journaling – Clear your mind, focus your energy.
- 30–40 minutes of exercise or movement – A strong body supports a strong mind.
- 1 hour for personal growth – Read, listen to a podcast, or learn something new.
- 1 connection-focused action – Call a mentor, message a friend, engage in a community.
- 1 fun or adventurous activity – Crypto should support your lifestyle, not consume it!

These simple habits compound over time and create mental resilience, clarity, and confidence—all crucial traits for thriving in the volatile crypto market.

Your Mindset Will Make or Break You in Crypto

Let's be real—crypto can be a wild ride. Prices can skyrocket overnight or plummet in minutes. If you let fear and greed control you, you'll end up making impulsive decisions that could cost you big time.

Instead of reacting emotionally, the best traders and investors think strategically. They see the bigger picture, stick to their plans, and trust the process.

Reprogramming Your Core Beliefs for Wealth

Your deepest beliefs about money and success shape every financial decision you make. If you've ever thought:

"I'll never be wealthy."
"I'm just not good with money."
"Money is hard to earn."
"Rich people are greedy."
"I don't deserve financial success."

…then these **limiting beliefs** could be **holding you back** without you even realising it.

The good news? **You can reprogram them.**

From Limiting Beliefs to Empowering Beliefs

Old Belief	New Belief
"I'll never be wealthy."	"I can create abundance in my life."
"I'm not good with money."	"I can learn to manage and grow my wealth."
"Money is the root of all evil."	"Money is a tool for freedom and opportunity."
"I don't deserve to be wealthy."	"I am worthy of financial success."
"Rich people are greedy."	"Many wealthy people use their resources to create positive change."

Pro Tip: Write down these empowering beliefs and repeat them daily. Your mind is like a computer—what you program into it determines what comes out. If you shift your beliefs, you'll start making decisions that align with wealth and success.

The 1% Rule—How Small Changes Lead to Big Results

Success doesn't come from huge overnight changes—it comes from small improvements every day.

Take James Clear's Atomic Habits as an example. He tells the story of the British Cycling Team, who couldn't win a major competition for years. Instead of trying to overhaul everything at once, they focused on getting just 1% better every day.

Within five years, they dominated the sport—winning Olympic gold medals and Tour de France titles.

The same applies to building wealth. Small, consistent improvements in your mindset and habits will lead to massive results over time.

Instead of stressing about getting rich overnight, focus on what you can do today.

Strategies to Reprogram Your Mindset for Wealth

Changing your beliefs isn't just about thinking positive—you need actionable strategies to make these shifts stick.

1. Affirmations—Rewrite Your Inner Narrative

- Write down and repeat empowering beliefs every day.
- Example: "I am a disciplined investor who makes smart decisions."

2. Evidence Collection—Find Proof That It's Possible

- Seek real-life examples of people who have built wealth starting where you are.
- Learn from success stories and remind yourself it's achievable.

3. Visualisation—See Your Future Success

- Picture yourself already achieving your goals.
- Feel the excitement, the confidence, the success—make it real in your mind.

4. Actionable Steps—Turn Thoughts into Reality

- Align small daily actions with your reprogrammed beliefs.
- Example: If you believe "I can learn to trade successfully," commit to learning 30 minutes a day.

Overcoming Fear and Self-Doubt

Fear of failure is the biggest thing holding most people back from financial success. But failure isn't the opposite of success—it's part of the journey.

Instead of worrying, "What if I fail?" ask, "What if this is my breakthrough?"

How to Push Through Fear:

✓ Identify Your Triggers – Journal about what scares you most about money and investing.
✓ Reframe Your Narrative – Replace fear-based thoughts with empowering affirmations.
✓ Visualise Success – Picture yourself thriving despite past failures.

Take Action Today

Here are three things you can do right now to start shifting your mindset:

- **Practice Gratitude** – Instead of focusing on what you lack, appreciate what you have.
- **Surround Yourself with Growth-Minded People** – Your environment shapes your success.
- **Invest in Yourself** – Whether it's a book, course, or trading group, continuous learning builds confidence and skill.

You've Laid the Foundation—Now Get Ready to Level Up!

Your mindset is now in the right place—**next, we dive into the psychology of money**.

Tomorrow, we'll cover:

✓ How emotions like **fear and greed** impact your financial decisions.

✓ Strategies to **stay calm, rational, and in control**—no matter how the market moves.

✓ How to start your **Trading Journal**—your secret weapon for long-term success.

Get excited—Day 2 will change how you think about trading forever!

Start small. Think big. And remember it all begins within.

Day 2

The Psychology of Money

Understanding emotional biases like fear and greed. Strategies to stay rational in trading.

Action tip: Start a "trading journal" to log decisions and emotions. https://belikelisa.com/bll-trading-journal/

Daily Habits Checklist

- 5 minutes of gratitude practice or affirmations.
- 15–20 minutes of market research or skill-building.
- 30–40 minutes of physical activity or stretching.
- 1 intentional act of kindness or networking outreach.
- 1 creative or relaxing activity (art, reading, or exploring something new).

Master Your Emotions, Master Your Wealth

When it comes to building wealth—especially in crypto—emotions can be your biggest asset or your worst enemy. It's not just about knowing the right strategies or reading the charts correctly. If you can't master the psychology of money, you'll struggle to make smart decisions when the market gets volatile.

Think about it: How many times have you seen people panic-sell at the bottom of a crash or FOMO into a pump, only to watch prices drop moments later?

The key to financial success isn't just strategy—it's emotional control.

Today, we're going to dive into how fear and greed influence your trading decisions, how to stay rational, and how to develop the mental resilience needed to thrive in the market.

How Emotions Can Make or Break Your Success

Let's look at Paul Tudor Jones, one of the most successful traders in history.

Early in his career, he let greed control him—holding onto a losing trade, hoping for a turnaround. That decision cost him dearly. But instead of giving up, he learnt from his emotional mistakes and committed to mastering the psychology of trading.

How did he do it?

✓ He set strict stop-loss limits to control risk.
✓ He followed his trading plan, even when emotions tried to take over.
✓ He kept a trading journal to track his decisions and spot emotional patterns.

By removing emotions from his trading, he turned his career around and built a fortune. His story proves one thing—if you master your emotions, you master the market.

So, how do you do that?

Understanding Emotional Biases

Your emotions drive financial decisions, often more than logic does. Two of the biggest emotional biases in trading are fear and greed.

Fear

This shows up as hesitation, panic-selling, or avoiding risk altogether.

Example: You buy Bitcoin at $50,000. It drops to $48,000, and fear kicks in. Instead of waiting for a market recovery, you panic-sell—only to watch it rebound to $55,000.

This reaction happens all the time. **Fear clouds judgment, leading to impulsive decisions.**

Greed

Greed makes traders **chase profits without thinking rationally**.

Example: A coin you bought has doubled in price. Instead of securing some profits, you hold on, convinced it will keep rising. Then the market reverses, and you lose all your gains.

Both **fear and greed** can **destroy your trading strategy** if you don't recognise them in time.

How to Stay Rational and In Control

1. Create a Clear Plan

Before you enter any trade, **define your strategy**:

✓ Your **entry point**
✓ Your **exit plan** (both profit-taking and stop-loss levels)
✓ Your **risk management approach**

By having a plan in place, **you take emotion out of the equation.**

Day 3

Overcoming the Scarcity Mindset

Break Free from Scarcity Thinking

Have you ever found yourself saying, "I just don't have enough money to invest" or "What if I lose everything?" If so, you've experienced the scarcity mindset—a way of thinking that keeps people stuck in fear and limitation, unable to see the opportunities right in front of them.

In the world of crypto, where innovation is constant and wealth can be built from even the smallest investments, a scarcity mindset will hold you back more than anything else.

Today, we're going to challenge this way of thinking, reframe your beliefs around money, and shift your perspective to one of abundance—because the truth is, opportunities are everywhere if you're willing to see them.

What is the Scarcity Mindset?

A scarcity mindset is when you focus on what you don't have instead of what's possible. It creates a cycle of fear, hesitation, and inaction.

It sounds like this:

"I can't afford to invest in crypto; I might lose everything."
"I missed the Bitcoin boom—there's no point starting now."
"I don't know enough to get involved."

These thoughts keep you **stuck**—playing it safe, waiting for the "perfect" moment (which never comes), and watching from the sidelines as others take action.

It should sound like this instead:

"Every small step I take now is a building block toward financial freedom."
"There are always new opportunities in crypto—I just need to educate myself."
"The best way to learn is by getting started."

How Scarcity Thinking Holds You Back

A scarcity mindset affects your ability to grow wealth. Here's how:

- You hesitate to invest, even after doing your research.
- You focus on short-term gains instead of long-term potential.

- You avoid risk entirely, thinking it's "safer" to do nothing.
- You believe financial success is for "other people," not you.

But here's the reality: The crypto market thrives on bold decisions, innovation, and those willing to take action. If you stay stuck in fear, you'll always feel like you're missing out.

A Real-Life Example: The Power of an Abundance Mindset

One of the most inspiring examples of abundance thinking is Chris Gardner, the real-life inspiration behind *The Pursuit of Happiness*.

Gardner started with nothing—homeless, jobless, and with a child to care for. He could have focused on what he lacked, but instead, he reframed his struggles into opportunities.

Instead of saying, "I'm homeless," he said, "I'm between homes."
Instead of believing, "I have nothing," he said, "I have skills I can develop."

He stayed focused on long-term success, learning everything he could and refusing to let his circumstances define him. Eventually, he built a career in finance and became a millionaire.

The lesson? Your reality isn't fixed—it's shaped by how you see it. The difference between opportunity and limitation is simply perspective.

How to Shift from Scarcity to Abundance Thinking

If you've spent years thinking in terms of scarcity, shifting to abundance won't happen overnight. But with small, consistent changes, you can retrain your brain to see opportunities instead of obstacles.

1. Reframe Limiting Beliefs

Your thoughts create your reality. If you constantly tell yourself "there's not enough," your brain will find reasons to support that belief.

Swap these limiting beliefs for empowering ones:

Scarcity Thought	**Abundance Reframe**
"I don't have enough money to invest."	"I can start small and build over time."
"There's no opportunity left in crypto."	"New innovations are happening every day."
"If I take a risk, I might lose."	"Every risk I take is a chance to learn and grow."

Scarcity Thought	Abundance Reframe
"I'm not good enough to succeed in this."	"Success is a skill, and I can develop it."

2. Celebrate Small Wins

Every step forward counts. Whether it's buying your first fraction of Bitcoin, learning a new strategy, or making your first profit, acknowledge your progress.

A great example of this mindset in action is ThousandtoMillions.com—a community built around starting small and growing wealth over time. Big wins come from consistent action.

3. Visualise Your Success

Your mind responds better to images and emotions than just thoughts.

Try this: Close your eyes and imagine your future success. What does financial freedom look like for you? How does it feel?

Create a vision board with images of your goals—your dream home, travel destinations, or even screenshots of your ideal portfolio. Seeing your future success reinforces the belief that it's possible.

4. Practice Gratitude

Gratitude rewires your brain for abundance.

Instead of focusing on what's missing, focus on what you already have:

✓ The ability to learn about crypto.
✓ The internet giving you access to unlimited knowledge.
✓ The fact that you're already investing in your future by reading this book.

Action Tip: Start an "Abundance Tracker"

Each day, write down three things you're grateful for and one opportunity you noticed—whether or not you acted on it.

Example entry:

Gratitude: "I'm grateful for my ability to learn new skills."
Opportunity: "I saw a promising new crypto project—I'll research it further."

This habit trains your brain to see possibilities instead of limits.

Daily Habits Checklist

- 5 minutes of gratitude practice or affirmations.
- 15–20 minutes of crypto news or market analysis.
- 30–40 minutes of physical movement or exercise.
- 1 meaningful action toward a financial goal (research, trade, networking).
- 1 joyful activity that inspires creativity or relaxation.

Your mindset is your greatest asset—train it well, and abundance will follow.

What's Coming Next: Patience—The Wealth Builder's Superpower

Now that you're breaking free from scarcity thinking, it's time to develop one of the most underrated skills in crypto patience.

When you let go of scarcity thinking, you start seeing possibilities instead of obstacles.

Crypto is full of opportunities—but only for those who are open to seeing them.

So, start thinking bigger, taking action, and embracing abundance. Your success story is just beginning.

Day 4

Patience – Wealth Builder's Superpower

If there's one trait that separates successful investors from those who struggle, it's patience. In the fast-paced world of crypto, where prices can skyrocket and crash within minutes, staying calm and composed isn't just a virtue—it's an essential skill.

The truth is, impulsive trading ruins portfolios, while long-term, well-planned strategies lead to real wealth. The most successful traders and investors aren't the ones making constant trades—they're the ones who think ahead, plan meticulously, and wait for the right opportunities to unfold.

So, let's talk about why patience is your greatest asset in wealth creation, the dangers of impulsive trading, and how you can develop the discipline to let your money grow over time.

Why Patience is Critical in Crypto and Investing

One of the biggest misconceptions in crypto is that you need to act fast to win big. While it's true that crypto moves quickly, the most profitable strategies are based on patience, not speed.

Here's how patience helps you succeed:

You ride the waves, not fight them. Crypto is volatile. Prices move up and down all the time. A patient investor knows the long-term trend matters more than short-term fluctuations.

You avoid FOMO (Fear of Missing Out). When prices are pumping, it's tempting to jump in without thinking. But buying high out of panic often leads to losses.

You let compounding do the heavy lifting. Wealth isn't built overnight—it grows over time. Even small, consistent investments can turn into significant gains if given enough time.

ThousandToMillions.com is a prime example of how small steps lead to massive financial success through long-term strategies.

Patience allows you to step back, assess the bigger picture, and make decisions based on logic, not emotions.

The Dangers of Impulsive Trading

If patience builds wealth, impulsiveness destroys it.

Here's how impatience shows up in trading:

Chasing Green Candles – You see a coin skyrocketing and buy in at the peak, only to watch it drop.

Panic Selling – The market dips, and fear kicks in. You sell, locking in a loss—only for the price to rebound.

Overtrading – You make unnecessary trades just to feel like you're "doing something," often leading to poor decisions and losses.

Each of these behaviours is driven by emotion, not strategy.

The key to breaking free from impulsive trading is discipline and planning.

Real-Life Story: How Dan Zanger Turned $10,775 into $18 Million

Let's talk about one of the most remarkable trading success stories.

Dan Zanger, a self-taught trader, holds the world record for the largest percentage gain in a personal portfolio over a 12-month period.

He started with just $10,775 in the late 1990s and, through disciplined trading and patience, grew it into $18 million in 18 months.

How did he do it?

He waited for high-probability setups. No chasing pumps, no reckless trading—just waiting for the right moment.

He reinvested his profits strategically. Compounding his gains turned small wins into massive success.

He had strict discipline. He followed his risk management plan, cutting losses quickly and letting winners ride.

The takeaway? Compound trading isn't about hitting home runs. It's about small, disciplined actions that allow your wealth to multiply over time.

The potential is limitless when you combine patience, a clear strategy, and the willingness to reinvest your profits.

How to Cultivate Patience in Your Trading

So, how do you develop the **self-discipline** to wait for the right opportunities instead of making impulsive decisions?

Have a Clear Plan

Before you enter any trade, decide:

Your entry price – At what price are you willing to buy?
Your exit price – When will you take profits?
Your stop-loss – How much are you willing to lose before cutting your losses?

When you have a plan, you don't let emotions make decisions for you.

Use Tools to Reduce Emotion

Crypto markets move fast, but you don't have to chase them.

Use limit orders. This allows you to set your buy/sell prices in advance—removing emotion from the equation.

Set alerts instead of watching charts all day. Checking your phone every five minutes will only make you anxious and more likely to trade on impulse.

Automate your investing. Using a dollar-cost averaging (DCA) strategy removes emotional decision-making from when to buy.

Knowing where the market is—bull or bear—also helps. When you understand the bigger picture, you don't let short-term moves shake you.

Zoom Out – Think Long Term

Short-term market moves don't matter when you're investing for the long run.

Look at historical trends—most successful investors buy during fear and hold through volatility.

Bitcoin, Ethereum, and other major cryptos have gone through multiple crashes—yet they've continued to rise over time.

The secret? Zoom out. The long-term trend is what matters most.

Learn from the Pros

Some of the most successful investors in the world attribute their wealth to patience, not just skill.

- Warren Buffett – Built his fortune by focusing on long-term investments rather than quick gains.

- Paul Tudor Jones – Stresses the importance of discipline and waiting for the right setups.
- Dan Zanger – Used strict risk management and patience to compound his portfolio.

Success leaves clues—study those who have mastered patience and follow their lead.

Action Tip: Set Up a Limit Order Today

Pick a crypto asset you're interested in.
Research a strategic buy or sell price.
Create a limit order to remove emotions from your trading.

This one simple action will teach you the power of patience firsthand.

Daily Habits Checklist

- 10 minutes of market research or analysis.
- 20 minutes of reading or watching content on long-term investors.
- 30–40 minutes of exercise to clear your mind.
- 1 deliberate action to strengthen your trading strategy (like setting up a limit order).
- 1 fun activity to help you unwind and recharge.

Patience Isn't Just a Virtue—It's a Superpower

Patience is the difference between chasing losses and building wealth.

- It stops you from making emotional mistakes.
- It lets you ride market cycles instead of reacting to them.
- It allows your investments to compound and grow exponentially.

The most successful crypto investors aren't the ones who trade the most—they're the ones who trade with the most patience.

Day 5

Your Relationship with Risk

Risk. Just the word alone can stir up emotions—excitement, fear, anticipation, or anxiety. Whether you're the type to dive headfirst into new opportunities or someone who hesitates before making a move, understanding your relationship with risk is essential in crypto.

Unlike traditional markets, where prices move steadily, crypto is a wild ride—full of sharp spikes and sudden dips. Without a solid understanding of risk management, it's easy to get swept up in the highs and lows, making impulsive decisions that could cost you everything.

So, let's break it down. Today, you'll learn:

The difference between risk tolerance and risk capacity.
How to create a risk management plan that protects your wealth.
Why understanding risk doesn't mean avoiding it—but using it wisely.

If you can master risk, you can master long-term wealth building. Let's get into it.

Risk Tolerance vs. Risk Capacity

People often confuse risk tolerance with risk capacity, but they're very different—and understanding both is crucial.

Risk Tolerance – Your Emotional Threshold for Risk

Risk tolerance is how much risk you can emotionally handle before it causes you stress. It's about your mindset—not your money.

Ask yourself:

- Can I handle watching my portfolio drop 30% without panicking?
- Do I get excited by high-risk, high-reward opportunities, or do they make me nervous?
- If I lose money on a trade, do I stay calm or rush to "make it back"?

Someone with a high risk tolerance can stay level-headed during volatility. Someone with a low risk tolerance might panic-sell at the first sign of a dip.

Remember: Just because you have a high risk tolerance doesn't mean you should take reckless risks.

Risk Capacity – How Much You Can Actually Afford to Lose

Risk capacity is the financial side of risk—how much you can afford to lose without it affecting your essential expenses or long-term financial goals.

Ask yourself:

- If I lost this investment, would it impact my ability to pay rent or bills?
- Do I have a backup plan if this trade doesn't go my way?
- Am I investing money I can afford to lose, or am I putting my life savings on the line?

Even if you have a high risk tolerance, your risk capacity should always dictate your investment decisions.

For example:

You might love high-risk, high-reward strategies (high risk tolerance), but if you don't have enough financial backup, you shouldn't be going all-in on volatile assets (low risk capacity).

Balancing risk tolerance and risk capacity is the key to smart investing.

Real-Life Story: How Risk Management Turned a Loss Into a Fortune

Let's talk about **Ray Dalio**, one of the world's most successful investors and the founder of Bridgewater Associates.

Early in his career, Dalio made a bold market prediction—and it went horribly wrong. He lost nearly everything and had to start over from scratch.

Instead of quitting, Dalio learnt from his mistakes. He realised that success wasn't about being right all the time—it was about managing risk so that mistakes wouldn't wipe him out.

He developed a strategy that combined risk tolerance and risk capacity, focusing on:

- Diversification – Spreading investments across different assets to minimise risk.
- Calculated moves – No more gut-feeling predictions, only data-driven decisions.
- Risk limits – Understanding how much risk was too much and setting rules to protect himself.

Today, Dalio runs the largest hedge fund in the world, managing over $150 billion. His biggest lesson?

"He who lives by the crystal ball will eat shattered glass."

In other words—no one can predict the market perfectly, but if you manage risk well, you don't need to.

How to Create a Risk Management Plan

If you want to succeed in crypto, you don't just need a trading strategy—you need a risk management plan. Here's how to build one:

1. Assess Your Finances

Before making any trade, ask yourself:

- How much of my portfolio can I afford to allocate to high-risk assets like crypto?
- What percentage of my investments should stay in safer, more stable assets?

A good rule of thumb: Never invest more than you can afford to lose.

2. Set Clear Goals

Your risk level should match your investment goals.

Short-term gains? You might take on more risk with high-volatility assets.

Long-term wealth building? You may prefer steady, calculated growth with lower risk exposure.

Define your goal, and your risk strategy will follow.

3. Diversify Your Investments

We've all heard the saying: "Don't put all your eggs in one basket."

This applies tenfold in crypto.

- Diversify across different assets – Bitcoin, Ethereum, altcoins, stablecoins.
- Consider a mix of short-term trades and long-term holdings.
- Don't just invest in one industry—explore multiple sectors within crypto (DeFi, NFTs, Layer 1 projects, etc.).

Diversification reduces risk while still allowing you to capture market gains.

4. Use Stop-Loss Orders

A stop-loss order is a pre-set price at which your asset will automatically sell if the price drops too low.

Why it matters: It removes emotion from the equation and protects you from devastating losses.

Set a stop-loss based on your risk tolerance and risk capacity.

For example:

If you're comfortable with a 10% loss, set a stop-loss 10% below your entry price.

Stop-loss orders act as your safety net—use them wisely.

5. Stick to Position Sizing Rules

Smart traders never go all-in on a single trade. Instead, they risk only a small percentage of their portfolio on any one trade.

A common rule among professional traders: Risk no more than 1-2% of your total portfolio on a single trade.

Example:

You have a $10,000 portfolio.
Instead of betting $5,000 on one trade, you risk just $100–$200 per trade.

This approach protects your capital while still allowing for growth.

Action Tip: Create Your Personal Risk Profile

Take 15 minutes today to assess your risk tolerance and risk capacity. Write it down.

- Ask yourself:
  How much can I afford to invest in high-risk assets?
- How do I react to market volatility—calmly or emotionally?
- What's my primary investment goal?

Use your answers to guide every trading decision moving forward.

Daily Habits Checklist

- 15 minutes to assess your finances and risk tolerance.
- Research one new risk management tool or strategy.
- 30–40 minutes of physical activity to boost mental clarity.
- Review your trading journal to identify patterns in how you handle risk.
- Enjoy a fun or relaxing activity to keep your mindset balanced.

Risk Isn't Something to Fear—It's Something to Master

Risk is part of the game—but if you understand it, you control it, not the other way around.

- High risk doesn't always mean high reward.
- Low risk doesn't always mean safety.
- The key is finding the balance that works for you.

With a solid risk management plan, you can grow your wealth while protecting what matters most.

Day 6

Setting SMART Financial Goals

Have you ever felt like you're investing aimlessly buying crypto because it "feels right" or reacting to market hype without a clear strategy? If so, you're not alone. Many people enter the crypto world with high hopes but no structured plan, making it easy to get distracted by volatility, FOMO, or short-term losses.

The secret to long-term success? SMART financial goals.

Having a clear, structured plan keeps you focused, reduces emotional decision-making, and helps you track progress effectively. Without a goal, you're just drifting through the market. With a goal, every move you make has purpose.

Today, we're diving into how to set SMART goals, why they work, and how you can apply them to your crypto journey.

How Visualisation Turned Dreams into Reality

Before we get into goal setting, let's talk about Jim Carrey—one of the world's most successful actors, but someone who started from nothing.

Before he made it big, Carrey was a struggling comedian, barely making ends meet in Hollywood. But instead of giving up or waiting for luck to strike, he did something unconventional but powerful.

He wrote himself a cheque for $10 million for “acting services rendered” and post-dated it for five years in the future.

Every day, he carried that cheque in his wallet, visualising his success, reinforcing his belief, and aligning his actions with that vision.

The result? Just before the date on the cheque, he landed his breakout role in Dumb and Dumber—and got paid exactly $10 million.

This is the power of seeing your success before it exists and letting that vision guide your actions.

Setting SMART goals works the same way. They turn abstract dreams into concrete, actionable steps.

What Are SMART Goals (And Why Do They Work)?

A SMART goal is:

Specific – Clearly define what you want to achieve.
Measurable – Set criteria for tracking progress.
Achievable – Make sure it's realistic given your resources.
Relevant – Align it with your bigger financial vision.
Time-bound – Set a deadline to create urgency.

Why does this matter? Because vague goals lead to vague results.

Compare these two:

"I want to invest in Bitcoin." (Too vague—how, when, and how much?)

"Accumulate 1 BTC by December 2025 by investing $500 monthly into Bitcoin, reviewing my progress quarterly, and adjusting as needed."

Now THAT'S a goal. It's structured, measurable, and actionable.

SMART goals help you stay on track, measure success, and stay committed even when markets get rocky.

Example SMART Goal in Crypto

Let's break down a realistic, achievable crypto goal.

Goal: *"I want to accumulate 1 BTC by December 2025."*

Is it SMART? Let's check:

- Specific: BTC accumulation (not just "investing in crypto")
- Measurable: $500/month investment plan
- Achievable: Fits within a budget—no unrealistic expectations
- Relevant: Aligned with long-term financial independence
- Time-bound: Set to complete by December 2025

See how this provides clarity, direction, and accountability?

With this plan, you know exactly what to do every month—no second-guessing, no emotional investing.

And here's the best part: If the market crashes, you don't panic—you just stick to your plan and keep accumulating.

How to Set Your Own SMART Financial Goals

Step 1: Define Your Financial Vision

Ask yourself:

- What do I want to achieve with crypto?
- Am I looking for long-term wealth, passive income, or short-term gains?
- How much risk am I comfortable with?

Your goals should align with your bigger financial vision—not just hype or market trends.

Step 2: Break It Down Into Smaller, Manageable Steps

Big goals can feel overwhelming. That's why breaking them down into smaller milestones makes them easier to achieve.

Example:
Instead of saying, *"I want to make $100,000 in crypto,"* break it down into:

- *"I'll invest $1,000/month into Bitcoin and Ethereum."*
- *"I'll stake 10% of my portfolio in DeFi for passive income."*

- *"I'll trade a small portion (5%) of my portfolio for higher returns."*

Each step brings you closer to the big goal without feeling overwhelming.

Step 3: Write It Down and Keep It Visible

Studies show that people who write down their goals are 42% more likely to achieve them.

Put your goal somewhere visible—on your phone, desk, or trading journal.
Review it daily.
Track progress regularly to stay accountable.

A written goal isn't just an idea—it becomes a commitment.

Daily Habits Checklist

- Write down one SMART financial goal.
- Spend 10–15 minutes reflecting on your "why" for financial freedom.
- Engage in 30–40 minutes of exercise to keep your mind sharp.
- Connect with someone who inspires you in your financial journey.
- Celebrate progress—reward yourself for sticking to your goals.

Success in crypto isn't about luck—it's about having a plan and sticking to it.

Action Tip: Review and Adjust Your Existing Goals

Do you already have financial goals? Take 10 minutes today to review them.

If they're vague, adjust them to fit the SMART framework.
Make sure they are clear, measurable, and time bound.

Example: Instead of saying, *"I want to make money trading,"* say,
"I will trade with a strict 2% risk per trade and aim for a 10% monthly portfolio growth over the next six months."

The more specific your goal, the easier it is to achieve.

Your Goals Are Your GPS to Success

Without goals, you're wandering aimlessly in the market. But when you set clear, structured, and achievable targets, you:

Stay focused during market volatility.
Make decisions based on logic, not emotion.
Track progress and adjust your strategy as needed.
Feel confident knowing you're working toward a bigger financial future.

Crypto is a powerful tool for wealth building—but only if you have a plan.

So, take control of your future. Set your SMART goal today and start working toward it!

Day 7

Visualise Your Wealth Before It Exists

If you want to build wealth, you need to see it first—not just on charts or spreadsheets, but in your mind.

The most successful people in the world—from athletes to business moguls—use visualisation to turn their dreams into reality. It's not just about wishful thinking; it's about mentally preparing yourself to succeed, reinforcing your goals, and taking the right actions to achieve them.

When it comes to crypto investing, visualisation can help you:
Stay focused on long-term success (instead of getting caught up in daily price swings).
Align your actions with your financial goals.
Build the confidence to invest with clarity, rather than fear or doubt.

Today, we're going to dive into how visualisation can fast-track your wealth-building journey, plus an exercise to create your own vision board or wealth journal.

How Visualisation Creates Financial Freedom

Let's look at someone who mastered the art of visualisation—Oprah Winfrey.

Long before she became one of the most successful entrepreneurs in the world, Oprah was just another struggling talk show host with a vision far bigger than her reality. She didn't just dream of financial freedom—she mentally rehearsed it every single day.

She imagined:
Hosting her own show and inspiring millions.
Living a life of abundance and success.
Using her wealth to make an impact.

By visualising her success as if it had already happened, Oprah's actions naturally aligned with her vision. Today, she's worth over $2.5 billion, proving that visualisation—combined with action—is a powerful wealth-building tool.

Success doesn't happen by accident. It happens because you prepare for it—mentally and physically.

The Science Behind Visualisation & Why It Works

Visualisation isn't just a motivational tool—it's backed by science.

Neuroscience research shows that when you vividly imagine a future event, your brain treats it as if it's already real. This activates the same neural pathways that fire when you actually experience success, making it easier for your brain to accept and work toward your goals.

Think of it like mental programming—if you keep reinforcing the idea of success, your brain naturally guides your decisions in that direction.

That's why professional athletes use mental rehearsal before a big game, and why the world's top investors keep their financial goals at the forefront of their minds.

Check out a few of my Instagram Posts

https://www.instagram.com/p/DDLtA2PhKS4/

https://www.instagram.com/p/DDVk5hqh2_q/

Visualisation Techniques to Solidify Your Goals

You don't need to be Oprah or an elite athlete to use visualisation. Anyone can do it. Here are two simple but powerful techniques to start using today:

1. Mental Visualisation

Take a quiet moment and close your eyes. Imagine:

- Your crypto portfolio in 6 months, 1 year, 3 years—how much have you accumulated? What coins do you hold?
- The lifestyle your financial success brings—where are you living? How do you spend your time?

- The feeling of achieving your goal—do you feel secure? Excited? Empowered?
- The impact your wealth has on your life and those around you—who are you helping?
- What opportunities have you unlocked?

The key is to engage your emotions. The clearer and more vivid the vision, the more powerful its effect on your mindset and actions.

Try this: Every morning, take 5 minutes to mentally rehearse your success—see it, feel it, believe it.

2. Create a Vision Board or Wealth Journal

A vision board is a physical or digital representation of your financial goals. It serves as a daily reminder of what you're working toward.

- How to create your vision board:
  Gather images, quotes, and words that represent your goals.
- Include crypto-related visuals (like Bitcoin, Ethereum, or passive income streams).
- Add lifestyle elements—travel, dream home, financial freedom.
- Arrange them on a board (physical or digital) where you can see them every day.

Alternatively, start a wealth journal.

In your journal, write about:

- Your financial goals—where you want to be and by when.
- Your visualisation exercises—what success looks and feels like.
- Your progress and achievements—big or small, celebrate every win.

By reinforcing your vision daily, you'll train your brain to expect success—and take the necessary steps to make it happen.

Your Action Plan

Take 10 minutes today to mentally visualise your ideal financial future.
Create your vision board or start a wealth journal.
Commit to reviewing your vision every morning and evening to stay focused on your crypto goals.

Daily Habits Checklist

- Spend 10 minutes visualising your ideal financial future.
- Dedicate 20–30 minutes to exercise to maintain focus and clarity.
- Work on your vision board or wealth journal.
- Connect with someone who supports your goals (send a message or plan a call).

- Engage in a fun activity that brings you joy and recharges your energy.

Action Tip: Make Visualisation a Daily Habit

Visualisation only works if you do it consistently.

- Every morning, take a few minutes to focus on your vision.
- Revisit your vision board or wealth journal regularly.
- Remind yourself daily: Your success is already happening—it's just a matter of time.

Success starts in the mind, if you can see it, you can achieve it.

Visualise It Until It's Real

The most successful people saw their success long before it happened.

Oprah. Jim Carrey. Top traders. Elite athletes.

Now, it's your turn.

See your wealth. Feel it. Believe it. And then take the steps to make it real.

WEEK 2

Crypto Trading Strategies

Day 8

The Basics of Technical Analysis

Let's start with a story from me! Lisa N Edwards

The volatility was overwhelming when I first transitioned from traditional markets to crypto trading. In the stock market, a 2% daily swing might cause headlines, but 10%, 20%, or even 30% moves in a single day are not uncommon in crypto. It felt like stepping into a storm, where everything was faster, more intense, and unpredictable. It was nail-biting, so I know how you feel!

Coming from the relatively stable pace of traditional markets, this level of volatility was daunting. I had to unlearn old habits and quickly adapt to the new environment. The key for me was shifting my mindset:

- **I embraced the volatility** as an opportunity rather than a threat.
- **I learned to read charts with precision**, using candlesticks, support/resistance levels, and trends to make informed decisions.
- **Risk management became my anchor**, ensuring I never overexposed myself to the wild swings of the market.

Crypto taught me to act decisively but never impulsively. With each trade, I gained confidence, realising that volatility isn't something to fear—it's a powerful tool when approached with the right strategy. Today, I see those wild swings as opportunities to grow wealth, not threats to my portfolio.

The Basics of Technical Analysis

Technical analysis (TA) is a powerful tool that helps traders make informed decisions by studying price charts and patterns. Whether you're a day trader or a long-term investor, mastering the basics of TA is essential for spotting opportunities and managing risks.

Here's what we'll cover today:

1. **Understanding Candlestick Charts**
2. **Identifying Support and Resistance**
3. **Recognising Trends**

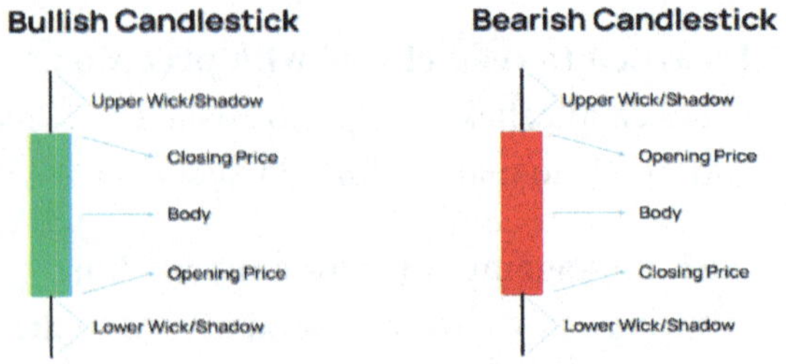

1. Understanding Candlestick Charts

Candlesticks are the building blocks of TA. Each candlestick represents price movement over a specific time frame.

- **Body**: The difference between the open and close price.
- **Wicks (Shadows)**: The highest and lowest price during the period.
- **Colour**: Green or white means the price closed higher than it opened, and red or black means it closed lower.

Candlesticks give you insights into market sentiment and potential reversals.

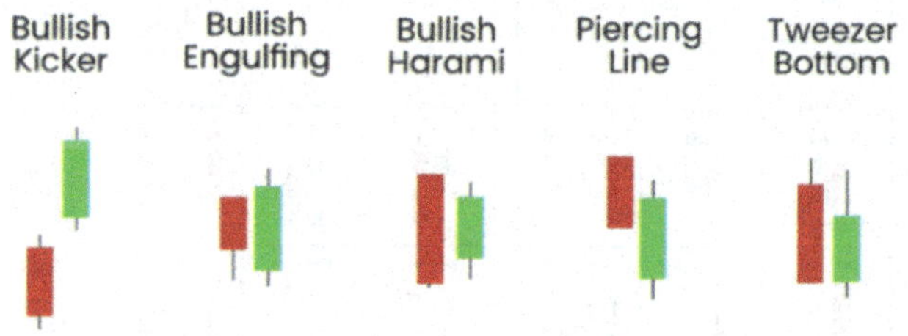

Candlestick Patterns Cheat Sheet

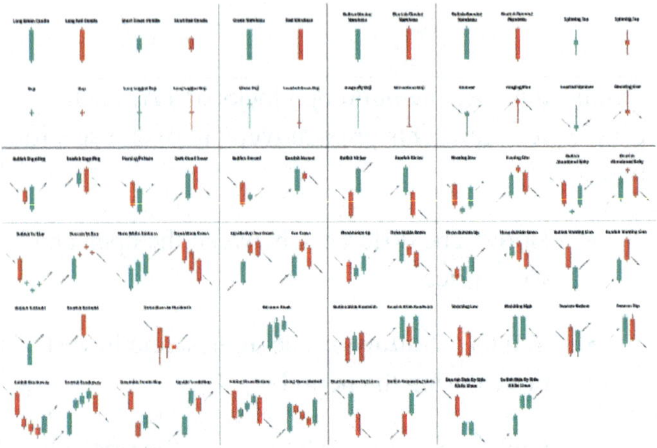

Candlestick Patterns Cheat Sheet for Cryptomarkets

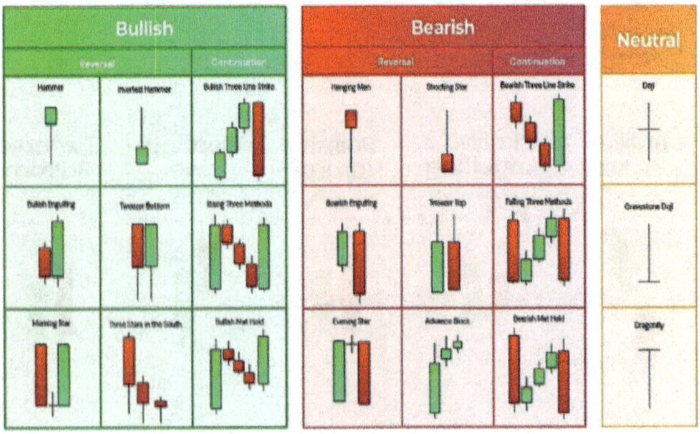

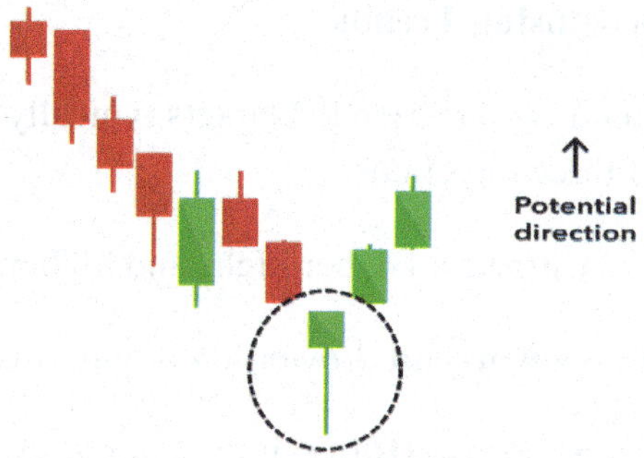

2. Identifying Support and Resistance

- **Support**: A price level where buyers tend to step in, preventing the price from falling further.
- **Resistance**: A price level where sellers dominate, stopping prices from rising.

Think of these levels as the market's floors and ceilings. Understanding them helps you plan entries, exits, and stop-loss orders.

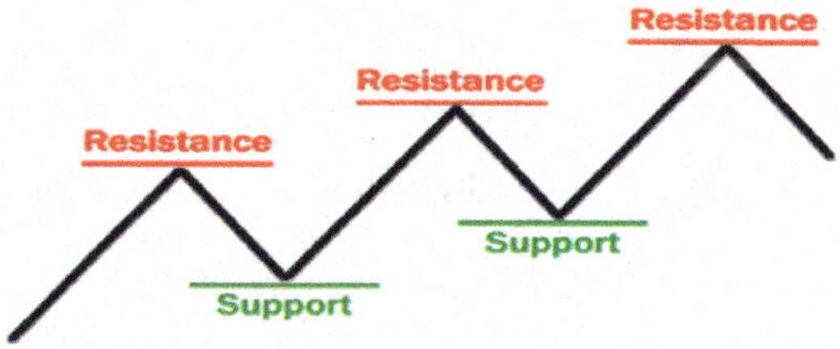

3. Recognising Trends

The trend is your friend! Markets typically move in one of three directions:

- **Uptrend**: Higher highs and higher lows.
- **Downtrend**: Lower highs and lower lows.
- **Sideways (Range)**: Price moves within a horizontal range.

Use trendlines and moving averages to identify the market's direction and plan your trades accordingly.

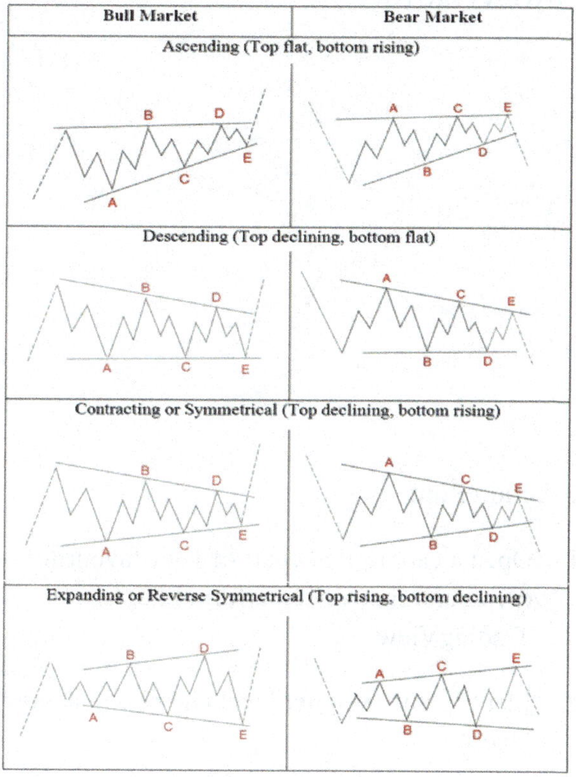

Guidelines

- • Corrective structure labelled as ABCDE
- • Usually happens in wave B or wave 4
- • Subdivided into three (3-3-3-3-3)
- • RSI also needs to support the triangle in every time frame
- • Subdivision of ABCDE can be either abc, wxy, or flat

MOVING AVERAGES

Your Action Plan

1. Open a candlestick chart of your favourite cryptocurrency on a platform like TradingView.

2. Identify one **support** level and one **resistance** level.

3. Look for the current **trend direction** and note any potential trade setups.

Daily Habits Checklist

- Spend 10 minutes reviewing candlestick charts.
- Practice drawing support and resistance levels on a chart.
- Exercise for 20–30 minutes to maintain focus and energy.
- Share your progress with a fellow crypto enthusiast or mentor.
- Enjoy a fun activity to reward yourself for your hard work.

Action Tip

Practice makes perfect. Set aside 15 minutes daily to analyse charts and mark trends. Start simple—focus on one coin or token and build your skills gradually.

Mastering technical analysis will help you navigate the crypto markets with confidence. Take it one step at a time, and remember, every great trader started with the basics.

Day 9: Fundamental Analysis for Crypto

- How to evaluate a project: team, utility, and tokenomics.
- Learn the best tools to use, like CoinMarketCap and Glassnode.

We're diving into a critical skill every crypto investor needs: fundamental analysis. If technical analysis helps you time your trades, fundamental analysis (FA) helps you decide *what to trade or invest in.*

Real-Life Story: How Don Turned Trading Signals into Life-Changing Wins

Meet Don, one of our success stories at *GettingStartedinCrypto.com.* Don started his journey as an everyday guy looking to make extra income. With a full-time job and limited time, he decided to trade using our signals. At first, he approached it cautiously, following the guidance and managing his risk carefully.

As his confidence grew, so did his results. With his profits, Don bought his wife her dream kitchen—a gesture that brought joy to his family and showed him the power of disciplined trading. But he didn't stop there. Don continued to trade consistently, reinvesting his earnings. Today, he's paid off his house and bought new cars for his family—thanks to his dedication and intelligent trading decisions.

Don's story is proof that you don't need to be a financial expert to succeed in crypto trading. Anyone can create life-changing results with the right tools, guidance, and a disciplined approach.

Fundamental Analysis for Crypto

The crypto market moves fast, and not all projects are created equal. FA helps you evaluate the quality and long-term potential of a project by analysing key aspects like:

1. **The Team**
2. **Utility and Use Cases**
3. **Tokenomics and Supply Dynamics**

1. The Team

Behind every successful project is a capable and credible team.

- Who are the founders? Research their background, achievements, and reputation in the crypto space.

- Who are the advisors and backers? Projects supported by reputable investors or advisors often signal strong potential.
- Community Engagement: A responsive and transparent team is usually committed to the project's success.

2. Utility and Use Cases

A great project solves a real-world problem.

- What problem does the project address? The clearer and more practical the solution, the better.
- Adoption Potential: Is the technology or product used or integrated into the industry?
- Competitive Advantage: What sets this project apart from others in its niche?

3. Tokenomics and Supply Dynamics

The economics of the token can make or break a project.

- Total Supply vs. Circulating Supply: Check if the supply is inflationary or deflationary.
- Utility of the Token: What's the purpose of the token (e.g., governance, payments, staking)?

- Distribution: Avoid projects in which insiders hold a large percentage of tokens, as this can lead to price manipulation.

Tokenomics -How to Identify Strong Crypto Projects

Tokenomics (Token + Economics) explains how a crypto asset is structured financially.

Key Metrics to Evaluate a Crypto Project:

Supply Mechanics:

- Max Supply – Limited coins like Bitcoin (21M) can become scarcer over time.
- Inflationary vs Deflationary – Does the supply increase (Dogecoin) or decrease (BNB burns tokens)?

Utility & Demand:

What problem does the token solve? (e.g., ETH for gas fees, LINK for oracles). Is the project widely adopted? (Check active users, partnerships, integrations).

Holder Distribution & Vesting Schedules:

Does the team own too many tokens? High insider holdings can lead to dumping on investors.

Are tokens locked or released over time? Sudden unlocks can crash prices.

Your Tools for Fundamental Analysis

1. CoinMarketCap: Offers project details, market cap, and circulating supply.
2. Glassnode: Provides on-chain data like wallet activity and market trends.
3. Official Websites & Whitepapers: Dive into the source for in-depth understanding.
4. Social Media Channels: Monitor updates and community sentiment.

Your Action Plan

1. Pick one crypto project you're interested in.
2. Research its team, utility, and tokenomics using CoinMarketCap and the project's whitepaper.
3. Write down your findings in a **Trading Journal** and evaluate whether it's worth investing in.

Also check out the article in TheMoonMag.com for more in-depth information.

Daily Habits Checklist

- Spend 15 minutes analysing one project.
- Engage in a forum or community discussion about the project.
- Take a 30-minute walk or workout session to refresh your mind.
- Allocate time for a creative or personal growth activity.
- Celebrate progress with a fun or relaxing activity.

Action Tip

Before you invest in any project, ask yourself: *Would I buy this token if the price didn't move for a year?* This mindset ensures you're focused on value, not hype.

Onward to Success! Understanding the fundamentals separates speculative traders from informed investors. Make the time to dig deeper, and you'll build a portfolio with purpose and strength.

Day 10

Mastering Risk in Leverage Trading

Leverage trading is like a double-edged sword. It can multiply your gains, but it can also magnify your losses. The difference between those who thrive and those who get wiped out… Risk management.

If you don't have a solid risk strategy, the market will teach you one the hard way—and trust me, that's not a lesson you want to learn with real money.

Today, we're going to dive into:

- Position sizing – How much you should risk per trade.
- Stop-loss orders – The safety net that keeps your capital intact.
- Risk/reward ratios – Ensuring your wins outweigh your losses.

Get this right, and you'll protect your account while still capitalising on opportunities. Get it wrong, and you won't have capital left to trade. Let's make sure you're on the right side of that equation.

Key Risk Management Strategies

- Never invest more than you can afford to lose.
- Use Stop-Loss Orders – Automatically sell if the price drops too much.
- Diversify – Don't put everything into one coin or asset.
- Calculate Position Sizing – Only risk 1-2% of your capital per trade.

Why Risk Management is the Key to Longevity

Your capital is your lifeline in trading. Without it, you're out of the game.

A missed trade is temporary. A blown account is game over.

Many traders think the goal is to make money—but the real goal is to stay in the game long enough to make money consistently.

Here's why risk management is non-negotiable:

- A 50% loss requires a 100% gain to recover.
- Blowing up your account means starting over from scratch.
- Over-trading leads to emotional decisions, which lead to losses.

The best traders don't focus on making millions overnight—they focus on preserving capital so they can keep trading for years.

Real-Life Story: Without Capital, There's No Game

Let's talk about **Alex**, a trader who started with big dreams and an even bigger appetite for risk.

He was drawn to leverage trading—the idea of making 10x gains in a short time was too tempting to resist.

Alex made some big wins early on. He felt invincible. So instead of sticking to the 2% rule, he started risking 30–40% of his account on a single trade.

Then the inevitable happened. A series of market swings wiped out most of his capital.

Without capital, Alex had nothing left to trade with. The game was over.

But instead of quitting, he took it as a painful but valuable lesson.

✓ He adopted strict risk management rules.
✓ He only risked 1–2% per trade.
✓ He used stop-loss orders to protect himself from major drawdowns.

Over time, Alex rebuilt his account the right way. Today, his mantra is simple:

"Preserve capital above all. Profits will follow."

This is the mindset that separates traders who last in the game from those who get wiped out.

The Core Pillars of Risk Management in Leverage Trading

Position Sizing – Don't Bet the House

One of the biggest mistakes traders make… Going all-in on a single trade.

Rule of thumb: Risk no more than 2% of your capital per trade.

Example:
If your trading account is $5,000, you should never risk more than $100 per trade.

Even if a trade goes wrong, your account stays intact.

Stop-Loss Orders – Protect Your Downside

A stop-loss order is your safety net. It automatically exits your position if the market moves against you.

Why it matters: It removes emotion from your trading decisions.

BAD stop-loss placement: Setting it too close to your entry, getting stopped out on normal volatility.

GOOD stop-loss placement: Placing it at a level where your trade idea is invalidated.

Example Stop-Loss Setup:
You enter a Bitcoin trade at $30,000.
Your stop-loss is set at $29,500 (risking $500).
Your target price is $31,500 (potential reward: $1,500).

Risk/Reward Ratios – Make Your Wins Count

A winning trade means nothing if your losses are bigger.

Aim for a risk/reward ratio of at least 1:3 (risk $1 to make $3).

Example Trade Setup:

- Entry Price: $30,000
- Stop-Loss: $29,500 (Risk: $500)
- Target Price: $31,500 (Reward: $1,500)
- Risk/Reward Ratio: 1:3

What this means: Even if you only win 40% of your trades, you're still profitable because your wins are larger than your losses.

Bad traders focus on winning every trade. Good traders focus on making sure their wins outweigh their losses.

Your Action Plan

Open a demo trading account to practise leverage trading with risk management.
Start Here: PHEMEX Demo Account

Get a PHEMEX account for real trading when you're ready.
Register with PHEMEX - https://phemex.com/register?group=6270&referralCode=HLRVM8

Use a trading journal to log your position sizes, stop-loss levels, and risk/reward ratios.
Download a Free Trade Tracker

Evaluate your results weekly and adjust your approach as needed.

Daily Habits Checklist

- Spend 15 minutes refining your risk management strategy.

- Perform a quick market scan to identify low-risk, high-reward setups.
- Dedicate time to personal growth (e.g., studying market psychology).
- Engage in a fitness activity to clear your mind.
- Reward yourself with a small indulgence for staying disciplined.

Discipline is Your Edge

The most successful traders aren't the ones who win every trade—they're the ones who manage risk so well that their losses never take them out of the game.

Key takeaways:

✓ Risk no more than 2% per trade—protect your capital.
✓ Always use a stop-loss—never leave your trade unprotected.
✓ Stick to a strong risk/reward ratio—so your wins outweigh your losses.
✓ Avoid emotional trading—discipline beats impulse every time.

If you can master risk management, you're already ahead of 90% of traders.

Day 11

Mastering Market Cycles

If you've spent any time in crypto, you'll know it's a wild ride. One minute, prices are skyrocketing, and everyone's celebrating their moon bags. The next, the market is crashing, and the same people are panic selling at a loss.

But here's the truth: crypto isn't random chaos—it moves in cycles.

Understanding these cycles isn't just about reading charts—it's about predicting opportunities before they happen. If you can identify a bull market early, you'll ride the wave to massive profits. If you can spot a bear market before it wipes out portfolios, you'll protect your capital and set yourself up for the next run.

So today, we're diving into:

- Bull vs. Bear Markets – How to spot them before it's too late.
- Bitcoin's Historical Cycles – Why the past often predicts the future.
- The Four Phases of Every Market – Accumulate, Profit, and Repeat.

Once you understand market cycles, you'll never look at crypto the same way again.

Understanding Bull & Bear Markets

The 4 Phases of a Market Cycle

- Accumulation Phase – Smart investors buy in before hype builds.
- Markup Phase – Prices rise rapidly, FOMO kicks in.
- Distribution Phase – Smart investors take profits while new traders buy at all-time highs.
- Markdown Phase – Prices drop, panic selling happens, and the cycle resets.

How to Spot Market Cycle Shifts

✓ Look at historical Bitcoin halvings & previous cycles.
✓ Track market sentiment – extreme greed = risk!
✓ Follow on-chain metrics like whale movements & liquidity trends.

Learning to Read Charts is Like Learning a New Language

When I first started trading, looking at charts felt like decoding an alien language.

Candlesticks, trendlines, and indicators? They made no sense.

I kept asking myself:
"How do people actually understand this? Am I even cut out for trading?"

But here's what I learned: reading charts is just like learning a new language.

At first, it's overwhelming. But the more you practise, study, and immerse yourself, the more intuitive it becomes.

Here's how I broke it down:

- Step 1: Recognising Patterns – Support, resistance, and trendlines.
- Step 2: Understanding Trends – Moving averages and momentum shifts.
- Step 3: Using Indicators – RSI, MACD, and volume for deeper insights.

Once I stopped overcomplicating it, trading became my roadmap to financial freedom.

Want to see a real-world breakdown? Check out this Bitcoin 4-Year Cycle analysis:

Bitcoin Market Cycle Chart

Bull Markets: The Green Zones

A bull market is when prices are rising consistently, investor confidence is high, and money is flowing into the market.

Key characteristics:

- Higher highs and higher lows – The market keeps pushing upward.
- Increased trading volume – More people are buying in.
- Mainstream hype – Media attention skyrockets.

Historical Examples

Bitcoin's 2017 Bull Run:

- Started the year at $1,000.
- Hit $20,000 by December.
- Retail investors flooded in.

Bitcoin's 2021 Bull Run:

- Bottomed at $3,200 in early 2019.
- Peaked at $69,000 in November 2021.
- Institutions (Tesla, MicroStrategy) joined the party.

What happens next?

Once prices peak, smart money takes profits, and the market starts cooling down. This is where FOMO-driven traders get wrecked because they bought too late.

Bear Markets: The Red Zones

A bear market is the opposite—prices decline, investors panic, and fear dominates the market.

Key characteristics:

- Lower highs and lower lows – A consistent downtrend.
- Decreased trading volume – People are afraid to invest.
- Widespread negativity – The media declares crypto "dead" (again).

Historical Example

Bitcoin's 2022 Bear Market:

- Peaked at $69,000 in November 2021.
- Dropped below $20,000 in 2022.
- Fear and uncertainty drove mass sell-offs.

This is where wealth is made.

The best time to accumulate isn't in a bull market—it's during a bear market when prices are low, and fear is high.

The Four Phases of Every Market Cycle

Markets don't just go up or down randomly—they move through predictable phases.

Accumulation (Smart Money Buys)

- Prices are low, but confidence is returning.
- Institutional investors and experienced traders start buying.
- The average person is still too scared to invest.

Markup (Bull Market Begins)

- The trend shifts upward—prices start rising.
- Retail investors (everyday people) start buying in.
- FOMO kicks in, and prices accelerate.

Distribution (Smart Money Sells)

- Prices peak, and experienced traders take profits.

- The market is full of hype—everyone thinks it will "keep going up."
- New traders buy the top, unaware that the bull run is ending.

Markdown (Bear Market Begins)

- Prices start declining, and fear spreads.
- Retail investors panic-sell at a loss.
- Smart investors accumulate at low prices, preparing for the next cycle.

Money is ALWAYS made in a BEAR MARKET.
BUY RED, SELL GREEN—not the other way around.

The people who get rich in crypto aren't buying at all-time highs. They're accumulating in silence when nobody is paying attention.

Your Action Plan

Study past market cycles – Look at Bitcoin's 2017 and 2021 bull runs.
Monitor market sentiment – Pay attention to news, fear indexes, and investor confidence.
Adapt your strategy to the cycle phase – Accumulate in bear markets, take profits in bull markets.

Daily Habits Checklist

- Spend 15 minutes analysing the current market phase.
- Watch a documentary or read an article about past crypto cycles.
- Dedicate 30–40 minutes to exercise or mindfulness to stay grounded.
- Discuss market trends with a fellow trader or join a crypto group.
- Treat yourself to something relaxing—reward consistency.

Patience is the Key to Wealth

Crypto isn't a get-rich-quick scheme—it's a long game. If you understand market cycles, you'll never panic during bear markets, and you won't get greedy at bull market peaks.

Key Takeaways:

- Bull markets bring opportunities, but they don't last forever.
- Bear markets are scary—but they're the best time to accumulate.
- Smart money buys low and sells high—not the other way around.

Most people get trapped in FOMO and panic-selling. But if you can think like smart money, you'll always be one step ahead.

Day 12

The Power of Dollar-Cost Averaging (DCA)

If you've ever hesitated before buying crypto, wondering if the price will drop the second you hit "buy," you're not alone.

Trying to time the market perfectly is one of the biggest mistakes new investors make. It's impossible to always buy the bottom or sell the top, and those who attempt it usually end up missing out or making emotional decisions.

That's where Dollar-Cost Averaging (DCA) comes in.

This strategy removes the stress and guesswork from investing. Instead of making one big purchase and hoping for the best, you invest a fixed amount at regular intervals, no matter what the price is.

The result? Your average purchase price evens out over time, reducing risk and building your portfolio steadily.

Let's dive into how DCA can transform your approach to investing—whether you're new to crypto or looking for a strategy that keeps you in the game for the long haul.

Building Wealth with a Simple, Steady Strategy

I've had the privilege of helping countless people transform their financial lives through crypto, and one of the most effective strategies I teach is DCA.

Take Sarah, for example. She's a working mum who wanted to invest in crypto but felt overwhelmed by the market's ups and downs.

She kept asking:
"What if I buy and the price crashes?"
"What if I miss the best time to get in?"

Instead of trying to predict the perfect entry, Sarah set up a simple DCA plan—investing a fixed amount into Bitcoin, Ethereum, and a few promising altcoins every week.

- She stayed consistent, even when the market was down.
- She ignored the noise and trusted the process.
- She focused on the long-term, not daily price swings.

Over two years, her portfolio grew significantly—not because she chased trends or got lucky, but because she invested steadily and let time do the work.

Lesson? Real money is made when the market is red—not when it's at all-time highs.

Success in crypto isn't about luck—it's about having a plan, staying disciplined, and leveraging strategies like DCA to build wealth over time.

Why DCA Works (And Why You Should Use It)

The biggest reason traders lose money.

Emotions.

Fear and greed cause people to buy high and sell low—which is the exact opposite of what you should be doing.

DCA eliminates emotional decision-making by sticking to a structured plan.

The Three Major Benefits of DCA:

Reduces Emotional Decisions

- No more guessing when to buy.
- No more panic-selling when prices dip.
- No more FOMO-buying at the top.

Mitigates Volatility

- Instead of going all-in at one price, you spread your buys across multiple price points.

- This means you automatically buy more when prices are low and less when prices are high.

Builds Discipline and Long-Term Success

- Investing becomes a habit, not a one-time event.
- The longer you DCA, the better your average cost basis.

DCA removes the stress from investing and keeps you focused on long-term growth.

Real-World Example: How DCA Could Have Made You a Fortune

Let's say you started a DCA plan in January 2020, buying $100 worth of Bitcoin every week.

- You would have bought during the COVID crash when Bitcoin dropped below $5,000.
- You would have bought during the 2021 bull market when Bitcoin hit $69,000.
- You would have bought during the 2022 bear market when Bitcoin fell below $20,000.

By December 2025, your steady purchases would have resulted in a substantial portfolio—likely outperforming someone who tried to time the market.

And as of today, Bitcoin has just reached $100,000 USD—meaning your consistent investments would have turned into massive profits.

Use this DCA Calculator to simulate how much you could have made:
🔗 Bitcoin DCA Calculator

The lesson? Timing the market is hard. Time in the market is what makes you wealthy.

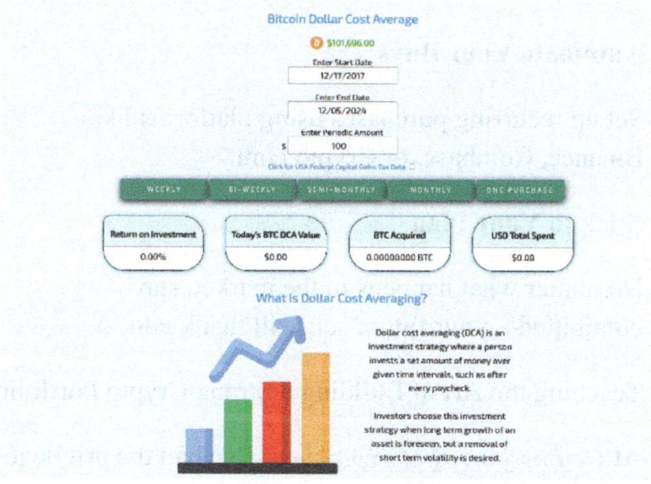

How to Start Your Own DCA Plan

Ready to put DCA into action? Here's how to get started:

Choose Your Asset

Pick a project you believe in long-term—Bitcoin, Ethereum, or other solid investments.

Set Your Interval

Decide whether you'll invest weekly, bi-weekly, or monthly.

Automate Your Buys

Set up recurring purchases using platforms like Binance, Coinbase, or Crypto.com.

Stick to Your Plan

No matter what happens in the market, stay committed—your future self will thank you.

Teaching the Art of Building a Strong Crypto Portfolio

At *GettingStartedinCrypto.com*, I've had the privilege of helping countless people transform their financial lives by building strong crypto portfolios. One of the most effective strategies I teach is Dollar-Cost Averaging (DCA).

Take *Sarah*, for example, a working mum who wanted to start investing in crypto but felt overwhelmed by market volatility and timing her entries. With my guidance, Sarah set up a simple DCA plan, which involves investing a fixed amount in Bitcoin, Ethereum and ALTs every week. She stayed consistent, even during market downturns, trusting the process. Real money is made when the market is red.

Over two years, Sarah's portfolio grew significantly, not because she chased trends but because she invested steadily and let time and compounding do the work. Today, she has a robust crypto portfolio and the confidence to make informed decisions, knowing her approach is built on a solid foundation.

Through my years of experience, I teach that success in crypto isn't about luck—it's about having a plan, staying disciplined, and leveraging strategies like DCA to build wealth over time.

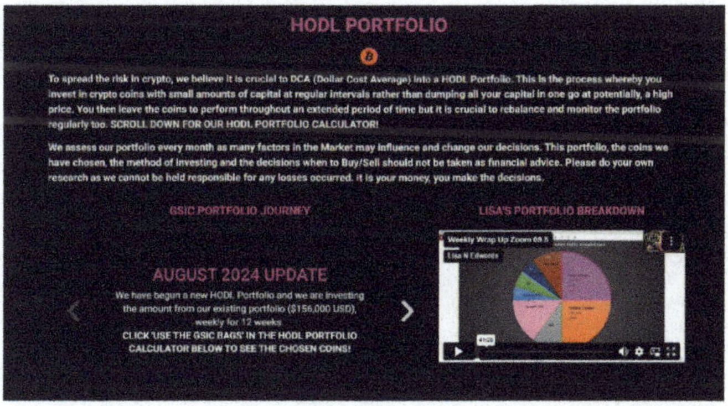

Daily Habits Checklist

- Spend 15 minutes reviewing your investment strategy and portfolio goals.
- Set up or optimise a DCA plan for your preferred crypto.
- Stay focused in a 30–40-minute workout or mindfulness activity.
- Reach out to a fellow investor to share insights or strategies.
- Do something enjoyable to celebrate your steady progress.

Final Thoughts: Slow and Steady Wins the Race

Key Takeaways:
DCA removes emotions from investing.

✓ Consistency beats trying to time the market.

✓ Long-term investing always outperforms short-term gambling.

DCA is the ultimate "set and forget" strategy. It allows you to build wealth without the stress of market timing. It's how smart investors accumulate during bear markets and profit in bull markets—without the emotional rollercoaster. If you want to build a strong, stress-free crypto portfolio, DCA is your best friend.

Day 13

How to Spot Trends and Stay Ahead

Have you ever felt like everyone else spots trends before you do?

By the time you hear about a project or a price movement, the big money has already positioned itself, and you're left deciding whether to jump in late or wait for the next opportunity.

Successful investors and traders don't chase pumps—they spot trends early and ride them before the masses catch on.

- That's exactly what today is about:
  Learning how to read market trends before they explode.
- Understanding key indicators like Moving Averages, RSI, and MACD.
- Combining technical analysis with news to perfect your timing.

Let's dive in and give you the edge you need to stay ahead of the market.

How Spotting Trends Transformed a Trader's Journey

Let's talk about John—a trader who started just like many others.

He was chasing hype, buying tops, and panic-selling bottoms. Every trade felt like a guessing game. Sometimes he won, but more often, he lost.

John decided to change his approach. Instead of reacting emotionally, he learned to analyse trends using Moving Averages, RSI, and MACD.

One of his key moments?

During a market dip, John noticed Bitcoin's RSI was oversold, while the MACD was showing bullish momentum. Instead of panicking like before, he entered a position with confidence.

- The market recovered.
- John's position grew 30% in value.
- That single trade changed his mindset forever.

Now, trend analysis is second nature to him. He combines technical indicators with market news to make informed, profitable decisions—instead of gambling.

And today, you're going to learn exactly how to do the same.

On-Chain Analysis – How to Track Whale Moves

On-chain analysis tracks real-time blockchain data to make better trading decisions.

Key On-Chain Metrics:

- Whale Wallets – Big investors control prices. Tracking their moves can indicate future trends.
- Exchange Flows – Large BTC or ETH deposits to exchanges may signal selling pressure.
- Network Activity – High transactions = more adoption (check Ethereum, Solana activity).

Tools for On-Chain Tracking:

Glassnode – Advanced blockchain analytics.

Whale Alert – Tracks big crypto transfers.

Etherscan – See real-time token movements.

Key Trend Indicators You Must Know

To spot trends early, you need the right tools. Here are three of the most powerful indicators every trader should use.

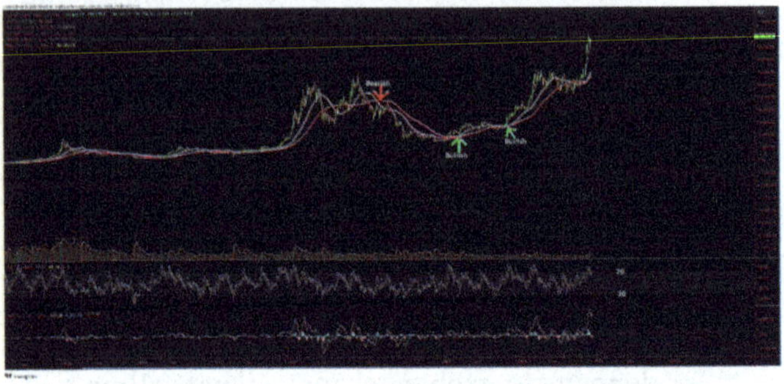

Moving Averages (MA): Your Market Compass

Moving Averages smooth out price fluctuations to give you a clearer picture of the overall trend.

Two key types:

- Simple Moving Average (SMA): Averages price over a set period (e.g., 50 or 200 days).
- Exponential Moving Average (EMA): Puts more weight on recent prices, making it more responsive.

How to use it:

- When **price is above the 200-day MA**, the asset is in an **uptrend**.
- When **price is below the 200-day MA**, it's a **downtrend**.

Pro Tip: Look for the "Golden Cross" (bullish) or "Death Cross" (bearish), where the 50-day and 200-day moving averages cross.

Relative Strength Index (RSI): Spotting Overbought & Oversold Conditions

RSI measures momentum by showing how strong or weak an asset's recent price movements are.

How to read RSI:

- Above 70 – Overbought (potential sell signal).
- Below 30 – Oversold (potential buy signal).

Example:

- Bitcoin's RSI drops below 30? That's a sign it might be undervalued.
- Ethereum's RSI hits 80? It could be due for a pullback.

Want to see RSI in action? Check out this TradingView chart:
Bitcoin RSI & Trend Example

MACD (Moving Average Convergence Divergence): The Trend Confirmation Tool

MACD helps identify momentum shifts in the market.

How to use MACD:

- MACD Line crossing above the Signal Line = Bullish (potential buy signal).
- MACD Line crossing below the Signal Line = Bearish (potential sell signal).

Example:

- If Bitcoin's MACD turns positive while RSI is oversold, it's a strong buy signal.

- If MACD turns negative while RSI is overbought, the market could be about to correct.

The key is to use these indicators together, not in isolation.

Combining Technical with News: The Winning Formula

Technical indicators are powerful, but **news can change the market instantly**.

Example 1:

- Bitcoin's RSI is oversold, and MACD is turning bullish.
- A major company announces they're adding Bitcoin to their balance sheet.
- Outcome: Bitcoin's price skyrockets.

Example 2:

- Ethereum's RSI is overbought, and MACD is turning bearish.
- Sudden regulatory news about a crackdown on staking hits the market.
- Outcome: Ethereum's price tanks.

Takeaway? Always combine technical indicators with real-world events to perfect your trade timing.

Practical Application: Putting It All Together

Want to apply what you've just learned? Here's how:

Step 1: Identify a crypto asset with a clear uptrend using Moving Averages.
Step 2: Check RSI and MACD to confirm momentum.

Step 3: Watch for news events that might accelerate the trend.

Use TradingView to apply these indicators:
🔗 Sign up for TradingView

The more you practise, the more second nature trend-spotting becomes.

Daily Habits Checklist

- Spend 20 minutes reviewing charts and applying trend indicators.
- Monitor news events for assets you're tracking.
- Dedicate 30–40 minutes to physical exercise to stay sharp.
- Connect with your community or a mentor for shared insights.
- Take time for a fun, relaxing activity to balance your day.

Trend Spotters Always Win

Key Takeaways:

- Stop guessing, start analysing use Moving Averages, RSI, and MACD.

- Technical indicators work best when combined with market news.
- The earlier you spot a trend, the more profitable your trades will be.

Most people chase trends after they've already moved. But not you.

You're learning how to spot trends before they happen—and that's the difference between traders who win and traders who lose.

Day 14

Common Crypto Trading Mistakes (And How to Avoid Them)

Every trader starts with enthusiasm and dreams of making life-changing money in crypto. But here's the harsh truth: most traders lose money—not because the market is unfair, but because they make costly mistakes.

Successful trading isn't just about knowing when to buy and sell—it's about knowing what NOT to do. The difference between the pros and the amateurs? The pros learn from their mistakes and never repeat them.

Today, we're diving into:
✓ The most common crypto trading mistakes.
✓ Real-life lessons from traders who learned the hard way.
✓ Mindful trading practices to keep you on the right track.

By the end of this, you'll trade with confidence—knowing how to avoid the traps that wreck most portfolios.

Trading Strategies – How to Win in Crypto

Three Trading Strategies That Work

- Scalping – Short-term trades, taking small profits multiple times a day.
- Swing Trading – Buying during dips and selling during peaks over days or weeks.
- HODLing – Long-term strategy where you hold onto assets for years.

How to Develop a Strategy That Fits You

- Choose a style based on time commitment & risk tolerance.
- Use technical indicators like RSI, MACD, and Moving Averages.
- Stick to a clear plan and avoid emotional trading.

How Mindful Trading Saved a Portfolio

Let's talk about Emily, a trader who started just like many others—excited, ambitious, and ready to make big gains.

But there was one problem: Emily was chasing pumps, entering trades on impulse, and overtrading.

- She bought tokens when they were already skyrocketing.
- She ignored fees, thinking they weren't a big deal.
- She panic-sold whenever prices dropped.

At first, she made some wins, but then the inevitable happened—she started losing more than she was making.

Emily took a step back.

- She created a trading plan with clear entry and exit points.
- She used stop-loss orders to protect her capital.
- She started keeping a trading journal to identify patterns in her decision-making.

The real turning point?

During a major bull run, a hyped project was going parabolic. Everyone was talking about it. FOMO was at an all-time high.

But Emily stayed disciplined. She didn't buy.

A week later, the price crashed. Many traders lost big, but Emily was safe. Instead, she used the downturn to accumulate quality assets at a discount.

That one decision saved her portfolio and set her up for massive gains in the next cycle.

Today, Emily is a confident, profitable trader because she learned one of the most valuable lessons in crypto:

Smart traders don't react. They strategise.

Top Crypto Trading Mistakes (And How to Avoid Them)

Let's break down the biggest trading mistakes that take down most beginners—and how to ensure you don't fall into the same traps.

Overtrading – The Fastest Way to Burn Your Capital

The Mistake:
Trading too often, without a clear plan, leads to higher fees, emotional decisions, and losses.

Why It Happens:

- You feel like you always need to be in a trade.
- You're trying to "make back" a loss quickly.
- You get bored and want action.

How to Avoid It:

- Stick to a clear plan—only trade when a setup meets your strategy.
- Set entry and exit points before you trade—don't change them mid-trade.
- Take breaks—sometimes, the best trade is no trade at all.

Pro Tip: Trading less often but with more precision leads to better results.

Ignoring Fees – The Silent Portfolio Killer

The Mistake:
Small transaction and withdrawal fees might seem insignificant, but over time, they add up and eat into your profits.

Why It Happens:

- You're making frequent small trades.
- You're using exchanges with high fees.
- You're not factoring in trading costs into your strategy.

How to Avoid It:

- Choose exchanges with competitive fees.
- Factor in trading fees when calculating risk/reward.
- Use limit orders instead of market orders (market orders often come with higher fees).

Pro Tip: If you're a frequent trader, look for exchanges that offer fee discounts for high-volume trading.

Chasing Pumps – Buying High, Selling Low

The Mistake:
You see a token skyrocketing, and FOMO kicks in. You buy at the top, only to watch it dump shortly after.

Why It Happens:

- The hype cycle makes you feel like you're missing out.

- Social media and influencers create fear of missing out (FOMO).

- You assume "this time is different"—it never is.

How to Avoid It:

- Wait for pullbacks. If a coin is pumping, chances are it will correct before making another move.
- Do your research. If you can't explain why a coin is pumping, don't buy it.
- Ignore the noise. Just because Twitter is hyping it up doesn't mean it's a good investment.

Pro Tip: The best time to buy was before the hype. The second-best time is after a correction.

FOMO (Fear of Missing Out) – The Emotion That Destroys Portfolios

The Mistake:
You see a coin trending, and you buy impulsively, ignoring your strategy.

Why It Happens:

- Social media makes you feel like everyone is making money except you.
- You don't want to miss out on "life-changing gains."
- You ignore logical entry points and buy emotionally.

How to Avoid It:

- Pause before entering any trade. If you're feeling FOMO, step back and reassess.
- Stick to your strategy. If a trade wasn't part of your plan yesterday, why are you considering it today?
- Remember, there will always be another opportunity.

Pro Tip: The best traders wait for the right moment instead of forcing trades out of FOMO.

Mindful Trading Practices

To stay disciplined and avoid costly mistakes, adopt these mindful trading habits:

- Before placing a trade, ask: *"Am I acting on logic or emotion?"* If it's emotion, pause and reassess.
- Use stop-loss orders to protect your capital and remove emotions from exits.
- Keep a trading journal (from Day 2) to track what's working and what's not.
- Take breaks—you don't need to be in the market 24/7.

Daily Habits Checklist

- Spend 10 minutes reflecting on past trades—successes and errors.
- Dedicate 30–40 minutes to physical exercise or a walk outdoors.
- Focus 1 hour on refining your trading strategy or learning a new skill.
- Reach out to a fellow trader or mentor for insights.
- Take time for an enjoyable activity to relax and recharge.

Trade Smart, Not Hard

Key Takeaways:

- Overtrading leads to burnout and losses.
- Ignoring fees can silently drain your profits.
- Chasing pumps and FOMO trading are recipes for disaster.
- Mindful, strategic trading is the path to long-term success.

Successful trading isn't about being perfect. It's about learning from mistakes and staying disciplined.

Avoid the traps of overtrading, FOMO, and emotional decisions, and you'll make smarter, more confident trades.

Trade smarter. Stay disciplined. And always have a plan.

WEEK 3

Advanced Strategies and Wealth Habits

Day 15

Making Your Money Work for You

Welcome to Week 3 where we take everything you've learned so far and step it up a level. The goal? Not just earning but growing your wealth sustainably.

Up until now, we've covered the foundations: mindset, risk management, and smart trading strategies. But the crypto market isn't just about trading—it's about building long-term wealth.

Today, we're diving into one of the most powerful ways to grow your crypto portfolio without constantly watching the markets—DeFi (Decentralised Finance) and staking.

Imagine earning passive income while you sleep—your crypto working for you, generating daily, weekly, or monthly returns.

Sound good? Let's break it down.

The Power of Simple Strategies & Consistency

Let me introduce you to Samantha, a single mum who felt financially stuck but was determined to create a better future.

She didn't have a background in investing, but she made one important decision: she started small, built consistent habits, and focused on long-term growth.

What did she do?

- She dedicated 15 minutes daily to learning about crypto.
- She set SMART financial goals (just like we covered on Day 6).
- She started Dollar-Cost Averaging (DCA) into Bitcoin, Ethereum, and selected altcoins every week.
- She discovered staking and DeFi, which allowed her to earn passive income on her existing assets.

At first, her earnings from staking and lending weren't life-changing—but they compounded over time.

Fast forward two years—Samantha had:

- Built a strong crypto portfolio.
- Used her staking rewards to pay off debt.
- Started a savings fund for her child's education.
- Taken her dream holiday, all while her investments continued to grow.

What was her secret? Consistency.

She didn't chase hype. She didn't gamble on random projects. She built real, sustainable wealth through steady strategies—and today, you're going to learn how to do the same.

Making Money Beyond Trading -Ways to Earn Passive Income in Crypto

- Staking – Earn rewards by locking up crypto (Cardano, Ethereum).
- Lending – Platforms like AAVE let you earn interest on idle assets.
- Liquidity Providing – Earn fees by providing liquidity on DEXs.
- Running a Masternode – Get paid to maintain a blockchain network.

Each method carries risks, so always research before investing.

Staking & DeFi – Earning Passive Income with Crypto

What is Staking?

Staking is the process of locking up cryptocurrency to support a blockchain network and earn passive rewards.

It's like putting your money in a high-interest savings account, but instead of a bank holding it, your crypto is locked up to support the blockchain network—and in return, you earn rewards.

Think of it as earning dividends on your crypto holdings.

Top Staking Platforms:

- Ethereum 2.0 Staking – Earn ETH by securing the network.
- Cardano (ADA) Staking – Low-risk passive income.
- Lido & Rocket Pool – DeFi platforms that allow flexible staking.

Is Staking Right for You?

Best for long-term holders.
Passive rewards with minimal effort.
Some platforms require a lock-up period.

Popular Staking Platforms & How They Work

Lido for Ethereum (ETH)

- Allows you to stake ETH while keeping liquidity (you get stETH tokens in return, which can be used in DeFi).
- Great for long-term ETH holders who want passive income.

Solana (SOL) Staking

- Solana's high-speed, low-cost network allows you to earn staking rewards with minimal fees.
- Perfect for those who believe in Solana's long-term growth.

Nexo Earn

- Stake or deposit your crypto and earn competitive interest rates.
- Supports stablecoins, Bitcoin, and Ethereum.
- Offers daily payouts on staked assets.

What is DeFi?

DeFi (Decentralised Finance) is an alternative financial system that cuts out banks and middlemen, letting you borrow, lend, trade, and earn interest—all on the blockchain.

Unlike traditional banks that keep most of the profits, DeFi platforms reward users directly.

Key DeFi Earning Opportunities

Lending & Borrowing – Platforms Like AAVE
Earn interest on your crypto by lending it out.
Borrow against your crypto without selling your assets.

Ideal for those who want liquidity without selling their holdings.

Liquidity Pools – Platforms Like PancakeSwap

- Provide liquidity for decentralised exchanges.
- Earn a share of trading fees as a reward.
- Higher risk, but higher potential returns.

Nexo – Passive Income on Crypto

- Deposit Bitcoin, Ethereum, or stablecoins.
- Earn daily compound interest.
- Borrow against your assets at low interest rates.

How to Start Earning Passive Income with DeFi & Staking

Step 1: Set Up a Secure Wallet

- MetaMask (for Ethereum-based staking and DeFi).
- Phantom (for Solana-based staking).
- Nexo or Binance (for easy staking & lending).

Step 2: Choose a Platform & Research

- Lido for ETH staking.
- Solana staking through your wallet.

- AAVE or Nexo for lending & earning interest.

Step 3: Start Small & Scale Up

- Begin with a small amount to understand how it works.

- Reinvest earnings to maximise compounding.

Step 4: Track Your Rewards

- Use tools like StakingRewards.com to monitor earnings.

Daily Habits Checklist

- Spend 10 minutes researching a DeFi protocol or staking option.
- Dedicate 30–40 minutes to physical movement to stay sharp.
- Spend 1 hour exploring staking rewards & calculating potential earnings.
- Connect with a fellow crypto enthusiast or join a DeFi-focused group.
- Celebrate reaching Week 3 with something fun or adventurous!

Let Your Crypto Work for You

Key Takeaways:
Staking and DeFi let you earn passive income instead of just holding crypto. Lido, AAVE, PancakeSwap, and Nexo are great places to start.
Always start small, research properly, and scale up over time.

Most people only focus on buying low and selling high, but the smartest investors let their assets work for them.

If you're serious about long-term wealth, passive income should be part of your strategy.

The best part? You're already ahead of 95% of investors just by understanding these concepts.

Day 16

Tax Strategies for Crypto Investors to Keep More of What You Earn

Let's be honest taxes aren't the most exciting topic in crypto. But if you're serious about long-term wealth, understanding crypto tax strategies is just as important as learning to trade or invest.

Why? Because a lack of tax planning can wipe out a significant portion of your gains.

Imagine making a life-changing trade, only to realise at tax time that you owe more than you expected. Or worse—you didn't keep records, and now you're scrambling to figure out what you owe.

Smart investors don't just make money—they keep more of it by staying compliant, tracking transactions, and using legal strategies to reduce their tax liability.

Crypto Taxes: What You Need to Know

Tax laws vary by country, but some universal principles can help you navigate the complexities.

The key is staying organised and proactive—because the last thing you want is a nasty surprise at tax time.

When Do You Owe Taxes? (Taxable Events)

Certain activities trigger taxable events, meaning you must report and pay taxes on your gains or income.

Crypto is taxable in most countries, and mistakes can lead to penalties.

Taxable Crypto Events:

- Trading – Swapping Bitcoin for Ethereum is a taxable event in many jurisdictions.
- Earning – Staking rewards, airdrops, and mining are taxable income.
- Selling for Fiat – Converting crypto to USD, AUD, or EUR triggers capital gains tax.

Ways to Minimise Crypto Taxes:

- Use FIFO or HIFO accounting – Different methods affect tax amounts.
- Hold for over 1 year – Many countries offer discounted long-term capital gains tax.
- Consider tax-free jurisdictions – Some countries (e.g., Portugal) don’t tax crypto gains.

The most common taxable events include:

Selling Crypto for Fiat

- Example: You sell Bitcoin for USD, AUD, or another fiat currency.
- You owe taxes on the profit (or loss) between your purchase price (cost basis) and selling price.

Swapping Cryptocurrencies (BTC to ETH, for example)

- Even if you don't cash out into fiat, swapping crypto is still a taxable event in most countries.
- The value of the crypto at the time of the swap determines your gain or loss.

Using Crypto for Goods or Services

- Spending Bitcoin or Ethereum to buy a product or service counts as a sale.
- You owe taxes on the difference between the crypto's value at the time of purchase and its original cost basis.

When Don't You Owe Taxes? (Non-Taxable Events)

Not every crypto transaction triggers a tax liability. Some activities are tax-free—unless specified otherwise by your country's tax laws.

Non-taxable events include:

Buying & Holding Crypto

- Simply buying and holding crypto is NOT taxable.
- Taxes only apply when you sell, swap, or spend it.

Transferring Crypto Between Your Own Wallets

- Moving crypto between your personal wallets or exchanges is NOT taxable.
- However, keeping records of these transfers is crucial for tracking your holdings.

Capital Gains Tax: Short-Term vs. Long-Term

When you sell or swap crypto, the profits are classified as capital gains—and they're taxed differently depending on how long you held the asset.

Short-Term Gains (Held for less than 1 year)

- Taxed at the same rate as your ordinary income (which is usually higher).
- Example: You bought Ethereum and sold it three months later for a profit—you owe short-term capital gains tax.

Long-Term Gains (Held for **more than 1 year**)

- Typically taxed at a lower rate, depending on your country's tax brackets.
- Example: You bought Bitcoin and held it for two years before selling—qualifying for lower long-term capital gains tax rates.

Pro Tip: The longer you HODL, the less tax you typically pay—another great reason to take a long-term approach!

Crypto as Income: Staking, Mining & Airdrops

Some crypto activities don't count as capital gains—they're classified as income and taxed accordingly.

You must report income if you earn crypto from:

Staking Rewards

- If you earn rewards from staking (e.g., Ethereum, Solana), the amount is taxed as income at the time you receive it.

Mining Rewards

- Crypto earned from mining is considered income, and you must report the value at the time it's received.
- Miners can also deduct expenses (like electricity and equipment costs).

Airdrops & Forks

- Free crypto received via airdrops or blockchain forks is taxable income.
- The value at the time of deposit determines how much tax you owe.

Why Record-Keeping is Essential

To simplify your tax reporting and avoid problems, you must track all transactions—whether buying, selling, or earning crypto.

Here's what you need to record:
✓ Date of transaction
✓ Type of transaction (buy, sell, swap, income)
✓ Crypto asset involved (e.g., BTC, ETH)

✓ Value in fiat at the time of transaction
✓ Fees paid

Recommended tax tracking tools:

Koinly.io – Automates crypto tax reporting.
CryptoTaxCalculator.io – Tracks transactions across multiple exchanges.

Pro Tip: Always download your exchange activity reports at the end of each year—it makes tax time MUCH easier.

Real-Life Story: How Smart Tax Planning Saved a Fortune

Let's talk about Michael—an early crypto investor who made huge gains but nearly got wrecked by tax season.

At first, he didn't track anything—just bought and sold crypto without considering taxes.

The problem? When tax season hit, he had no records, no transaction history, and no idea how much he owed.

What happened next?

- He scrambled to find old exchange records—a stressful nightmare.
- He owed more than expected because he didn't plan for taxes.

- He missed tax-saving strategies that could have reduced his liability.

Michael finally took control:

- Started tracking every transaction using Koinly.
- Learned about tax-loss harvesting to offset gains.
- Held crypto longer to qualify for lower tax rates.

The result? He cut his tax bill, reinvested the savings, and never stressed about taxes again.

Lesson? Taxes can be overwhelming—but staying organised makes all the difference.

How to Reduce Your Crypto Taxes

Want to pay less tax legally? Use these strategies:

- Harvest Losses – Sell underperforming assets to offset gains.
- Hold Long-Term – Benefit from lower long-term capital gains rates.
- Use Tax-Free Accounts – If applicable, explore crypto-friendly retirement or investment accounts.
- Get Professional Advice – A crypto-savvy accountant can help you save thousands.

Daily Habits Checklist

- Spend 10 minutes updating your crypto transaction records.
- Dedicate 30–40 minutes to exercise to stay focused.
- Research tax tools like Koinly or CryptoTaxCalculator.
- Discuss tax strategies with a professional or in a crypto community.
- Celebrate financial clarity with something enjoyable!

Taxes Don't Have to Be a Nightmare

Key Takeaways:

- Crypto taxes are unavoidable—but smart planning helps you keep more of your profits.
- Track every transaction to make tax season painless.
- Use tax strategies like loss harvesting & long-term holding to reduce your bill.

The best traders and investors don't just focus on making money—they focus on keeping it.

If you haven't already started tracking your crypto taxes, start today. Your future self will thank you.

Day 17

Diversification – More Than Just Bitcoin

If there's one golden rule in investing, it's "Don't put all your eggs in one basket."

Yet, time and time again, I see traders and investors go all in on a single asset, usually Bitcoin. While Bitcoin is the king of crypto, relying solely on it can leave you vulnerable to market swings.

Diversification is the key to long-term financial stability and growth.

It's not about maximising short-term gains—it's about protecting your portfolio, reducing risk, and ensuring steady returns regardless of market conditions.

How Diversification Saved a Portfolio

Let me introduce you to James, one of our members at GettingStartedinCrypto.com.

James entered the crypto market during the 2021 bull run. Like many new investors, he poured all his money into Bitcoin after watching it climb to new all-time highs.

At first, his portfolio skyrocketed. Every day, it seemed like Bitcoin was making him richer. But when the bear market hit, James' gains disappeared just as quickly as they came.

Frustrated and eager to change his strategy, he started diversifying:

✓ He added altcoins like Ethereum, Solana, and Polkadot.

✓ He held stablecoins like USDC and USDT to reduce volatility.

✓ He staked assets on platforms like Nexo to generate passive income.

✓ He invested in gold and blockchain-related stocks for added security.

The next time the market took a downturn; James' portfolio didn't collapse. While Bitcoin was struggling, his staking rewards kept earning, his stablecoins remained stable, and his diversified investments balanced out the losses.

Now, he no longer fears market crashes—he knows his portfolio is resilient.

And today, you'll learn how to do the same.

HODL PORTFOLIO

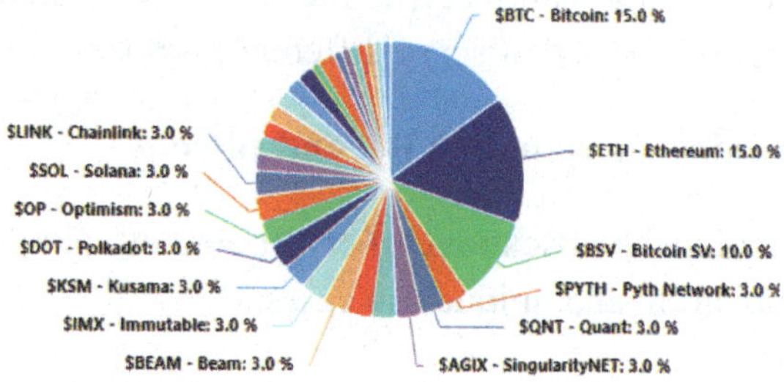

Why Diversify?

Crypto is volatile. One day, an asset can be up 100%, and the next, it can crash 50%.

Diversification protects your portfolio by:

- Reducing risk—so a crash in one asset doesn't destroy your entire portfolio.
- Increasing stability—mixing assets with different risk levels smooths out returns.
- Maximising long-term growth—while some assets drop, others may rise, keeping your portfolio strong.

The best investors don't just hold one asset—they spread their investments across multiple categories for maximum protection and profit potential.

Crypto Diversification: What to Consider

Diversifying within crypto means investing in different types of assets that serve different purposes.

Altcoins – Expanding Beyond Bitcoin

Bitcoin is the backbone of crypto, but altcoins bring innovation and unique use cases.

Consider adding:
Ethereum (ETH) – Smart contracts & DeFi leader.
Solana (SOL) – High-speed blockchain for NFTs and DeFi.
Polkadot (DOT) – Interoperability between blockchains.
SUI & SEI – Emerging networks with potential upside.
Tron (TRX) – Known for stablecoin transactions and DeFi.

Each of these has a unique role in the crypto ecosystem.

For more head to https://coinmarketcap.com/

Stablecoins – Your Safe Haven in Volatility

Stablecoins like USDT, USDC, and DAI are pegged to fiat currencies, meaning their value remains stable even when the market crashes.

How to use stablecoins effectively:

- Lock in profits without converting to fiat.
- Earn passive income through staking and lending.
- Hedge against downturns while keeping liquidity for new opportunities.

DeFi & Staking – Passive Income While You Wait

Why just hold crypto when you can earn from it?

Platforms like AAVE, Lido, Nexo, and PancakeSwap allow you to:

- Stake your crypto to earn rewards.
- Lend out assets and collect interest.
- Provide liquidity for decentralised exchanges.

Example: Staking Ethereum (ETH) on Lido can earn you passive rewards while you hold it for long-term gains.

NFTs & Metaverse Tokens – High Risk, High Reward

If you're open to more speculative investments, consider NFTs and metaverse-related tokens like:
Sandbox (SAND) – Virtual real estate & gaming.
Decentraland (MANA) – A decentralised metaverse platform.

Blue-chip NFTs – Established collections with long-term potential.

These assets can skyrocket in value, but they also carry high risk—so only allocate a small portion of your portfolio here.

Beyond Crypto: Why You Should Broaden Your Horizons

While crypto offers incredible growth potential, relying solely on it can be risky.

Consider balancing your portfolio with traditional assets like:

- Stocks – Invest in tech companies innovating with blockchain (e.g., Tesla, Coinbase).
- Precious Metals – Gold and silver act as hedges against economic uncertainty.
- Real Estate – Tokenised real estate or traditional property investments.
- Bonds – Low-risk assets that provide stability.

A balanced portfolio protects your wealth, no matter what happens in the markets.

How to Build a Diversified Portfolio

Diversification isn't random—it's about balancing risk and reward.

Here's a simple portfolio breakdown:

High-Risk, High-Reward (50%)

- Bitcoin, altcoins, or speculative NFTs.
- Higher growth potential but also more volatility.

Moderate Risk (30%)

- Staking projects, DeFi, and dividend-paying stocks.
- Earns passive income while holding long-term.

Low-Risk (20%)

- Stablecoins, bonds, or precious metals.
- Provides security and liquidity in downturns.

Adjust these percentages based on your risk tolerance and financial goals.

Daily Habits Checklist

- Spend 10 minutes visualising your diversified portfolio's success.
- Dedicate 30–40 minutes to learning about a new asset class.
- Research one new altcoin or stablecoin.
- Connect with another investor and share diversification tips.
- Reward yourself for taking another step toward financial mastery!

Diversification is Your Safety Net

Key Takeaways:

- Crypto is volatile—diversify to protect your wealth.
- Altcoins, stablecoins, and staking create balance.
- Beyond crypto, stocks, metals, and real estate provide stability.
- A well-structured portfolio keeps you profitable in any market.

If you want to build long-term wealth, diversification is non-negotiable.

Day 18

Preparing for the Next Bull Run

The crypto bull run is one of the most exciting, profitable, and emotionally charged events in the market.

It's the time when prices explode, media hype skyrockets, and newcomers flood into the space, driven by FOMO (Fear of Missing Out).

But here's the truth: the people who profit the most in a bull run aren't the ones who jump in late—they're the ones who position themselves ahead of time.

If you wait until Bitcoin is all over the news, you're already too late.

What Is a Bull Run?

A bull run is a prolonged period of rising prices and positive sentiment in the market. It's when opportunities abound—but only for those who are ready.

Positioning yourself ahead of time is the key to maximising gains during these explosive periods.

Real-Life Story: Fear and Greed at Play in Everyday Life

A classic example of fear and greed comes from *the dot-com bubble* of the late 1990s. While it's tied to investments, the emotional dynamics apply to everyday decisions.

Mark, a tech enthusiast, watched his colleagues and friends invest in dot-com startups. Stories of massive gains fuelled his greed. He believed, *"If they're making so much money, why shouldn't I?"* Without much research, Mark poured his savings into several tech stocks, driven by the fear of missing out (FOMO).

As the market continued to climb, greed took over. Even when his investments doubled, he resisted selling, thinking, *"What if it goes higher?"* Then came the crash. Stocks plummeted, and fear replaced greed. Instead of holding on or reassessing the fundamentals, Mark sold everything at a massive loss, terrified of losing everything.

Years later, Mark reflected on how his emotions—not logic—drove his decisions. Greed led him to invest blindly, while fear pushed him to sell in panic. He vowed never to let emotions dictate his choices again.

This has also happened to many traders in the crypto space, but they are not selling the market highs and sometimes holding to zero.

This story highlights how fear and greed aren't confined to trading—they influence career decisions, relationships, and even life's biggest financial moves. Recognising and managing these biases can lead to smarter, calmer, and more deliberate choices.

In Trading and Beyond

Fear and greed can cause impulsive decisions, but they can be managed with the right mindset and strategies. Whether in markets or in everyday life, self-awareness is key to staying rational and making better decisions.

How to Get Ahead Before the Next Market Surge

- Accumulate in the Bear Market – Buy when everyone else is fearful.
- Study Historical Bull Runs – Learn from past cycles.
- Build a Portfolio with High-Quality Projects – Focus on fundamentals, not hype.
- Have an Exit Strategy – Take profits at key resistance levels.

The next bull market will come—will you be ready?

How to Spot Early Indicators of a Bull Run

Market Sentiment:

- Watch for shifts in social media buzz and news coverage turning optimistic.
- Track metrics like the **Fear & Greed Index.**

Institutional Moves:

- Look for major corporations or funds announcing crypto investments.
- Monitor Bitcoin ETF approvals or regulatory updates that could boost adoption.

Volume and Momentum:

- Rising trading volumes and price breakouts from key resistance levels signal renewed interest.
- To confirm momentum, use tools like the RSI (Relative Strength Index) or MACD (Moving Average Convergence Divergence).

On-Chain Metrics:

- Track wallet activity: An increase in long-term holders accumulating Bitcoin or Ethereum can indicate bullish trends.

Use platforms like **Glassnode** to analyse inflows/outflows from exchanges.

https://www.cointree.com/learn/crypto-fear-and-greed-index/

Position Yourself for Future Gains

Build Your Bags:
Accumulate top assets like Bitcoin, Ethereum, or promising altcoins before prices climb. Use Dollar-Cost Averaging (DCA) to stay consistent.

https://www.bitcoindollarcostaverage.com/

Strengthen Your Knowledge:

Understand market cycles so you don't get caught off guard. Learn about historical bull runs (e.g., 2017 and 2021) and the events that triggered them.

Revise Day 13.

Set Alerts:

Use tools like **CoinGecko** or **TradingView** to set price alerts for key assets and stay informed.

Stay Liquid:

Allocate a portion of your portfolio to stablecoins (USDT or USDC) for quick trades when opportunities arise.

Action Tip: Create a Bull Run Checklist

Write down these steps to prepare:

1. Finalise your investment strategy for key assets.
2. Set profit targets and decide how much you'll hold vs. sell during a bull run.
3. Ensure you're following trusted news sources and tools.

Daily Habits Checklist:

- Spend 10 minutes researching historical bull runs.
- Dedicate 30–40 minutes to reviewing your portfolio and strategies.
- Set one price alert for a favourite crypto asset.
- Connect with a crypto-savvy friend or mentor to share ideas.
- Celebrate your progress—you're preparing for the future like a pro!

By preparing now, you're setting yourself up to thrive as the bull run continues. You'll be ready to make informed, confident decisions when the market takes off.

Day 19

Mental Resilience for Traders – Strengthen Your Mind for Success

Crypto trading isn't just about charts, indicators, and market trends—it's a mental game.

You can have the best strategies in the world, but if your mindset is weak, emotions will take over. And when that happens, fear, greed, and anxiety will lead to bad decisions.

Success in trading isn't about being perfect—it's about staying calm, disciplined, and rational no matter how volatile the markets get.

In this chapter, we're going to talk about mental resilience—how to manage stress, stay focused, and develop the discipline needed to succeed in crypto trading.

Why Mental Resilience is Non-Negotiable in Trading

Let's be honest: Crypto is an emotional rollercoaster.

One day, your portfolio is up 100%, and you feel like a genius. The next day, it's down 50%, and you're questioning every decision you've ever made. You see people posting huge gains on X(Twitter), and FOMO kicks in. A random news article causes the market to dip, and panic selling begins.

This cycle repeats over and over—and if you don't learn to control your emotions, it will control you.

Mental resilience isn't about being emotionless—it's about recognising emotions without letting them dictate your actions.

A strong mindset = a successful trader.

How I Manage Stress with Mindfulness, Yoga, Running, Reading, and Meditation

Stress is a constant companion in crypto trading and business, but I've learned that managing it effectively is the key to thriving instead of just surviving. Over the years, I've developed a personal toolkit of mindfulness practices that keep me centred and grounded, no matter what life or the market throws my way.

Every morning begins with meditation. Just 10 minutes of stillness sets the tone for my day. It's a moment to breathe deeply, clear my mind, and focus on my intentions. Meditation helps me stay calm and make thoughtful decisions, even when markets are volatile or deadlines loom.

Yoga is my go-to for physical and mental balance. Flowing through poses keeps my body strong and flexible and quiets the mental chatter. It's a practice that reminds me to be present, especially during challenging times. When I step off the mat, I feel more in tune with myself and ready to face the day with clarity.

When stress feels overwhelming, I lace up my running shoes and head outside or to the treadmill or elliptical. It is raining - nothing stops me! There's something therapeutic about hitting the pavement or trails. **Running** lets me release pent-up tension, and with every mile, I feel lighter, more energised, and better equipped to tackle challenges. And when I am outside - I have to return home, forcing me to detox those thoughts and stresses.

At night, I unwind with a good book. **Reading** allows me to step out of my world and into another, offering a fresh perspective and a sense of calm. Whether it's a novel, a biography, or a book on personal growth, it's my way of disconnecting from the constant hum of work and reconnecting with creativity and curiosity. And if you're looking to improve not only your trading emotions but also your trading knowledge of compound trading, grab my book!

BECOME A MILLIONAIRE IN ONE YEAR

https://thousandtomillions.com/

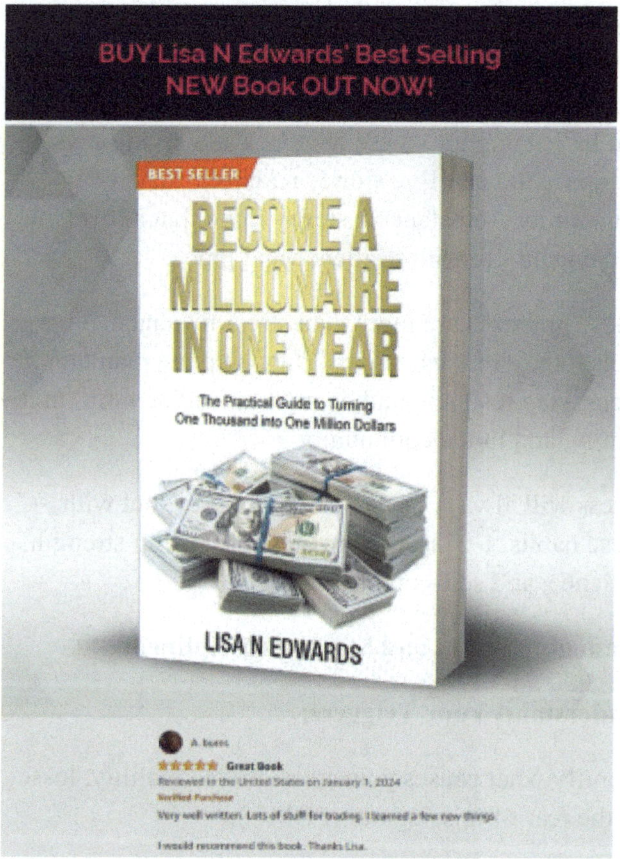

I use mindfulness techniques throughout the day, such as taking deep breaths before a meeting or pausing to savour a quiet moment. Mindfulness reminds me that I can choose calm and control my response even amidst chaos.

It's been extra challenging recently, as personal stresses and health issues have taken a toll. There were moments when the weight of it all felt overwhelming. But by leaning into these practices and giving myself the space to heal, I've slowly reached a state of equanimity—a balanced, steady mind that allows me to navigate life with resilience and grace.

These practices are more than stress management tools—they're my anchors. They help me maintain focus, stay resilient, and be my best self at work, in my family, and in the community.

Stress will always be part of the journey, but with these habits, I've learned to navigate it with strength, patience, and self-compassion.

Managing Stress and Staying Disciplined

Understand Your Triggers:

Identify what causes you stress: price volatility, losses, or the fear of missing out (FOMO).

Journaling your emotions can help you spot patterns and address them effectively.

Develop a Trading Plan:

Having predefined entry, exit, and stop-loss levels removes guesswork and reduces emotional decisions.

Stick to your strategy, even when the market tempts you to deviate.

Take Regular Breaks:

Overtrading or constant screen-watching increases anxiety. Schedule regular breaks to clear your mind and recharge.

Set Realistic Expectations:

Understand that losses are a part of trading. Focus on the long-term trend, not daily fluctuations.

Mindfulness Techniques for Traders

Deep Breathing Exercises:
When markets get turbulent, pause, and take five deep breaths. This activates your parasympathetic nervous system, reducing stress.

Meditation or Visualisation:
Spend 5–10 minutes daily visualising your goals or practising guided meditations to stay grounded.

Physical Activity:
Regular exercise reduces cortisol (the stress hormone) and improves decision-making.

Techniques for Staying Calm and Focused

Deep Breathing Exercises

When markets get turbulent, your body often responds like you're in physical danger—your heart races, muscles tense, and stress hormones surge. Deep breathing is a simple yet powerful tool to counteract this.

How It Works: Deep breaths activate the parasympathetic nervous system, responsible for relaxation and recovery. This process lowers your heart rate and calms the mind, making it easier to focus on rational decisions.

How to Practice:

Find a quiet space or simply sit in a comfortable position.

Breathe deeply through your nose for a count of four, expanding your diaphragm.

Hold your breath for a count of four.

Slowly exhale through your mouth for a count of six.

Repeat this cycle 5–10 times or until you feel more centred.
Use this technique anytime you feel overwhelmed or stressed, especially during market volatility.

Meditation or Visualisation

Meditation and visualisation are powerful techniques that can transform your mindset and trading performance.

Meditation:

Regular meditation trains your mind to remain calm and focused, even under pressure. Start with guided meditations or apps like Headspace, Calm, or Insight Timer.

A simple practice is focusing on your breath for 5–10 minutes daily. If your thoughts wander, gently bring your attention back to your breath without judgment.

Visualisation:

Visualisation is a mental rehearsal that helps solidify your goals. Imagine yourself succeeding in your trading strategy, sticking to your plan, and growing your wealth. The more precise and more detailed your vision, the more it motivates and builds confidence.

Spend a few minutes daily visualising your financial goals, such as hitting a savings milestone or reaching a specific portfolio value. Pair this with affirmations like, “I am disciplined and capable of achieving my trading goals.”

Physical Activity

Trading is often a passive activity, which can exacerbate stress and tension in the body. Incorporating regular physical activity into your routine has multiple benefits:

Reduces Cortisol: Physical activity lowers the stress hormone cortisol, helping you manage anxiety during high-pressure situations.

Boosts Endorphins: Exercise releases endorphins, the "feel-good" chemicals in your brain, improving mood and mental clarity.

Improves Decision-Making: Studies show that exercise enhances cognitive functions like decision-making, focus, and problem-solving, which are essential for successful trading.

Suggestions for Traders:

Quick Breaks: Incorporate short bursts of movement during your trading day, like stretching or a brisk 5-minute walk.

Daily Exercise: Aim for 30–40 minutes of moderate activity, such as jogging, yoga, or strength training.

Mind-Body Workouts: Activities like yoga and tai chi combine physical movement with mindfulness, providing dual benefits of stress reduction and focus.

Combining these techniques—deep breathing, meditation or visualisation, and regular exercise—you can cultivate a calmer, more resilient mindset supporting better trading decisions.

Action Tip: Create a Pre-Trading Ritual

Develop a short routine before trading that includes:

1. Reviewing your trading plan.
2. Practicing a mindfulness exercise, such as deep breathing.
3. Setting a clear goal for the session.

This ritual will help you approach trading with a calm and focused mindset.

Daily Habits Checklist:

- Spend 10 minutes practicing mindfulness or meditation.
- Dedicate 30–40 minutes to exercise or movement.
- Journal your trading decisions and emotions.
- Take one intentional break from your screen during market hours.
- Engage in stress-relieving activities like music, reading, or a hobby.

By building mental resilience, you're equipping yourself to handle whatever the market throws.

Day 20

Networking and Community Involvement – Your Crypto Tribe Awaits

Crypto moves fast—there are no snails here.

If you're new, it can feel overwhelming, like you're constantly playing catch-up. But the secret to staying ahead isn't just about learning technical skills or reading charts—it's about who you surround yourself with.

The crypto community is a goldmine of knowledge, connections, and opportunities—if you know where to look. Finding your tribe will help you spot trends early, stay motivated, and make better investment decisions.

So today, we're diving into how networking and community involvement can take your crypto game to the next level.

Why Networking Is Key

Expert Insights: Connect with experienced traders, developers, and analysts to gain valuable perspectives.

Early Access to Trends: Communities often discuss new projects and market shifts before they go mainstream.

Motivation & Support: Trading can feel isolating, but an active network provides encouragement and accountability.

Where to Get Started

Find Your Tribe

1. Discord: Join project channels or trading communities with active, value-driven discussions.

2. Twitter Spaces: Participate in live conversations with industry leaders, sharing insights and strategies.

3. Reddit: Explore subreddits like r/CryptoCurrency or r/Ethereum for diverse opinions and resources.

Follow and Learn from Influencers

You're here because you follow me https://linktr.ee/LisaNEdwards and are interested in the education I provide based on my years of trading experience and understanding of market psychology. Knowledge is wealth!

Here are some categories of experts to add to your list:

- Market Analysts: Traders sharing technical charts and strategies.
- Project Creators: Developers working behind the scenes of popular platforms.
- Educators: Thought leaders offering simplified resources for every level of expertise.

Engage and Contribute

1. Ask Questions: Use your community to clarify doubts and gather feedback.
2. Share Insights: Post what you learn or find interesting to spark discussions.
3. Expand Beyond Crypto: Cross-discipline groups like tech or investment clubs provide fresh perspectives.

Navigating Crypto Communities on X, Telegram, and Discord

The Good, The Bad, and The Cautious

Crypto thrives on vibrant communities, and platforms like X.com (formerly Twitter), Telegram, and Discord are where these conversations come alive. These hubs are invaluable for staying informed, learning from experienced traders, and discovering opportunities early—but they also come with risks.

The Good

X.com: A treasure trove for real-time updates and market sentiment.

- Influential traders and analysts share market insights, technical charts, and predictions.
- Educators simplify complex topics like DeFi, staking, or blockchain tech.
- News spreads fast, giving you a front-row seat to developments in projects and markets.

Telegram: Ideal for direct and fast-paced discussions.

- Many crypto projects maintain active channels where teams engage directly with the community.
- Groups often share early information about token listings, partnerships, or airdrops.
- You can ask questions, clarify doubts, and connect with like-minded enthusiasts.

Discord: The go-to for in-depth engagement and community building.

- Features channels for everything from beginner Q&As to advanced trading strategies.

- Regular AMA (Ask Me Anything) sessions with project founders and developers.
- A great place to join niche groups focused on NFTs, gaming, or specific blockchains.

TradingView Community: A Hub for Market Analysis

TradingView is more than just a charting platform; it's a thriving community of traders and analysts sharing their insights and strategies.

- Educational Content: Follow experienced traders who publish in-depth analyses, chart setups, and market predictions.

- Collaboration: Join discussions on specific assets or strategies in the comments section of published ideas.

- Customisation: Access and share custom indicators or strategies and learn how others use them to make decisions.

- Networking: Build connections with like-minded traders and receive feedback on your ideas.

While the TradingView community is generally well-moderated, remain cautious about users pushing paid services or guaranteeing profits. Stick to learning and collaborating with trusted contributors. You can create an account here TradingView

The Bad

While these platforms are great resources, they can also be breeding grounds for misinformation and scams.

- X.com: Fake accounts impersonating influencers or companies frequently promote phishing links or scams.
- Telegram: Scammers often infiltrate groups, posing as admins or trusted members, asking for personal wallet information.
- Discord: Direct messages (DMs) can be a trap with fraudulent investment offers, NFT drops, or fake giveaways.
- TradingView: While TradingView is an excellent tool, there are some pitfalls to be aware of:
- Overwhelming Content: The sheer volume of ideas and opinions can be confusing, especially for beginners, making it hard to discern quality analysis from noise.
- Paid Signal Promoters: Some users push paid services or signal groups with promises of guaranteed profits, which are often scams- no one can guarantee profits

- Bias Confirmation: It's easy to fall into the trap of following analyses that align with your existing bias, leading to less objective trading decisions.
- Unverified Users: Anyone can publish ideas, so not all content is accurate or reliable.

How to Stay Safe

- Verify Sources: Double-check information before acting on it. Follow official project accounts and avoid unknown links.

- Beware of "Too Good to Be True" Offers: Promises of guaranteed returns or free crypto are often scams.

- Turn Off DMs: Disable direct messages from strangers on Telegram and Discord to minimise risk.

- Stick to Known Communities: Join well-established groups with active moderation, like those at *GettingStartedinCrypto.com*.

The Bottom Line

Crypto communities on X, Telegram, and Discord can accelerate your learning and help you discover new opportunities. However, staying vigilant and exercising caution is essential to protecting your investments and personal information. Engage, learn, and connect, but always keep your guard up.

REMEMBER - IF IT IS TOO GOOD TO BE TRUE - IT PROBABLY IS!

Action Tip

Join a new crypto-focused community today. Start with one action: introduce yourself, ask questions, or contribute to a conversation. Networking is a two-way street, so give as much as you take!

Daily Habits Checklist

- Spend 15 minutes exploring a new crypto community (Discord, Reddit, or Twitter).
- Ask or answer one question in a crypto-focused group discussion.
- Follow 2–3 thought leaders in crypto and engage with their content.
- Dedicate 10 minutes to networking with like-minded individuals or collaborators.
- Reflect on one takeaway or a new connection made during your interactions.

Building relationships in the crypto space isn't just about learning—it's about finding allies in your journey to financial freedom.

Day 21

Closing: Your Wealth-Building Blueprint

- Summary of key lessons from the series.
- Free checklist or resource (e.g., a trading strategy template).
- Revisit lessons and start applying them today.

Congratulations! You've reached the final day of our 21-Day Crypto Mastery Plan. Over the past three weeks, you've gained powerful insights, actionable strategies, and a wealth-building mindset to take control of your financial future.

Today, we'll recap the journey, provide you with a free checklist to kickstart your trading plan, and set the stage for your next steps.

Your Wealth-Building Blueprint: Key Takeaways

Here's a summary of the critical lessons you've learned:

Week 1: Foundational Mindset and Financial Basics

- **Day 1:** Mastering your money mindset and overcoming limiting beliefs.
- **Day 2:** Recognising emotional biases like fear and greed while trading rationally.
- **Day 3:** Shifting from a scarcity to an abundance mindset for financial growth.
- **Day 4:** Developing patience as the cornerstone of long-term wealth.
- **Day 5:** Understanding risk tolerance vs. risk capacity. Creating a risk management plan.
- **Day 6:** Setting SMART financial goals to define your roadmap.
- **Day 7:** Using visualisation to align your mindset with your wealth goals.

Week 2: Core Trading and Investment Strategies

- **Day 8:** Learning the basics of technical analysis with candlesticks and trends.
- **Day 9:** Evaluating crypto projects through fundamental analysis.
- **Day 10:** Managing risk effectively in leverage trading with tools like stop-loss orders.
- **Day 11:** Navigating bull and bear market cycles with historical insights.
- **Day 12:** Leveraging Dollar-Cost Averaging (DCA) to mitigate volatility.
- **Day 13:** Spotting trends using indicators like moving averages and RSI.
- **Day 14:** Avoid common trading mistakes like overtrading and FOMO.

Week 3: Advanced Strategies and Wealth Habits

- **Day 15:** Generating passive income with staking and DeFi platforms like Nexo and PancakeSwap.
- **Day 16:** Navigating crypto taxes with smart record-keeping and reporting practices.
- **Day 17:** Diversifying beyond Bitcoin into altcoins, stablecoins, and traditional assets.
- **Day 18:** Preparing for the next bull run by recognising early indicators.
- **Day 19:** Building mental resilience through mindfulness and stress management techniques.
- **Day 20:** Tapping into the power of networking and community involvement in the crypto space.

Again, congratulations on completing the 21-Day Crypto Mastery Plan eBook! You've taken the first critical steps toward mastering the markets and building sustainable wealth. The journey doesn't stop here, it's only beginning. To keep momentum, here's some actionable advice to help you move forward with confidence:

Build Your Roadmap

Take time to revisit your goals and trading strategies. Write them down in your journal, break them into smaller actionable steps, and set realistic timelines. A clear plan provides direction and keeps you focused during uncertain times.

Embrace Consistency Over Perfection

Every successful trader starts with small, consistent steps. Whether practising technical analysis, contributing to a crypto community, or refining your risk management strategy, incremental progress leads to significant results.

Stay Curious and Keep Learning

The crypto world evolves rapidly. Dedicate at least 15 minutes daily to learning—explore new protocols, stay updated on market trends, or study advanced trading techniques. Knowledge compounds, just like your investments.

Reflect and Refine Regularly

Weekly reviews of your trades and strategies can uncover patterns and areas for growth. Use this time to celebrate small wins and adjust your approach where necessary. Growth comes from reflection and iteration.

Prioritise Emotional Discipline

Markets are volatile, but your mindset doesn't have to be. Use mindfulness techniques, take breaks, and stick to your trading plan to avoid decisions driven by fear or greed.

The Ultimate Trading Strategy Checklist

To help you implement what you've learned, I've prepared a **365-day Hardcover BeLikeLisa Trading Journal**—your go-to companion for creating and refining your trading strategy, staying disciplined, and maintaining motivation daily. This journal is packed with positive quotes, actionable tips, and thoughtful prompts to guide you through your journey to financial mastery.

Here's What It Includes:

- **Goal-Setting Prompts**
  Define your trading objectives with clear, actionable steps. Whether aiming for consistent monthly profits, a specific portfolio

value, or mastering a new strategy, this journal helps you focus on what truly matters.

- **Risk Management Tools**
  Learn how to calculate position sizes, set appropriate stop-loss levels, and effectively manage your risk/reward ratios to protect your capital.

- **Technical Analysis Quick-Reference Guide**
  Get an easy-to-use overview of essential indicators like moving averages, RSI, and MACD, along with tips on how to spot trends and key price levels.

- **Journaling Template**
  Record your trades, market observations, and emotional responses to maintain discipline and track patterns. Review your entries regularly to refine your strategies and build confidence.

- **Key Resources for Learning and Market Analysis**
  Discover must-have tools and platforms like TradingView, CoinMarketCap, Glassnode, and Nexo to analyse markets, manage your portfolio, and stay updated on crypto trends.

- **Daily Positive Quotes and Tips**
  Stay inspired with motivational quotes about life, success, and trading. Each day also

includes a practical trading tip or mindset hack to keep you focused and resilient, even in challenging markets.

- **Weekly Reflection Pages**
  Review your progress, celebrate wins, and identify areas for improvement with guided weekly prompts.

- **Actionable Monthly Goals**
  Plan your trading activities with monthly goal-setting sections designed to align with your overarching financial objectives.

Why You Need This Journal:

Success in trading is as much about mindset and discipline as technical skills. The **BeLikeLisa Trading Journal** is your roadmap to building habits that will lead to sustainable market success.

Start Your Journey Today:
Use this checklist and journal as your foundation. Every great trader started with a plan—this is yours!

Bonus: Share your progress in our community at **GettingStartedinCrypto.com** for tips, feedback, and exclusive insights.

Let's make your trading journey a success—365 days of focus, growth, & achievement await.

365 Day Hardcover BeLikeLisaTrading Journal

Your Next Steps: Turn Knowledge into Action

1. **Revisit the Lessons**: Go back to any email or lesson that resonated with you, and dive deeper into the topics you're most eager to master.

2. **Take Small Steps Daily**: Consistency is the key to progress. Start small, whether it's practising technical analysis, joining a new crypto community, or logging your first DCA investment.

3. **Join Our Growing Community**: The crypto journey is more rewarding with like-minded individuals. Join **GettingStartedinCrypto.com** today to connect with experienced traders, gain access to exclusive resources, and keep learning with our expert-guided courses.

Why You Need This Journal:

Success in trading is as much about mindset and discipline as it is about technical skills. The https://belikelisa.com/bll-trading-journal/ is your roadmap to building habits leading to sustainable market success.

365 Day Hardcover BeLikeLisaTrading Journal

Actionable Next Steps

Use the BeLikeLisa Trading Journal
With the journal, you can record your goals, track your trades, and reflect on your progress. It's your daily companion for cultivating discipline, staying inspired, and building wealth one step at a time.

Join a Crypto Community
Engage with like-minded individuals at *GettingStartedinCrypto.com.* Share insights, ask questions, and grow alongside a supportive network of traders and educators.

Commit to Daily Habits
Adopt these five key habits:

- Trade with a plan.
- Maintain emotional discipline.
- Set realistic expectations.
- Review and reflect weekly.
- Dedicate time to continuous learning.

Act on What You've Learned
Don't wait for the "perfect time." Start implementing what you've learned today set your first DCA

investment, analyse a chart, or explore a new staking platform.

Dream Big, Start Small
Remember, wealth-building is a marathon, not a sprint. Celebrate each milestone, no matter how small, and keep your vision focused on long-term success.

Habits to Live By for Trading Success

Always Trade with a Plan
Before entering any trade, take time to define your strategy. Identify your entry point, stop-loss level, and take-profit target, ensuring every action is calculated and intentional.

Maintain Emotional Discipline
Commit to sticking to your trading strategy, even during volatile market swings. Practice mindfulness to avoid emotional decisions driven by fear or greed.

Set Realistic Expectations
Focus on achieving steady, smaller gains rather than chasing risky "get-rich-quick" opportunities. Remember, long-term consistency beats short-term wins. ThousandtoMillions.com will teach you how!

Review and Reflect Regularly
Dedicate weekly time to reviewing your trading journal: note patterns, mistakes, and successful strategies to continuously improve your approach.

Keep Learning
Spend at least 15 minutes daily expanding your knowledge. Follow market updates, explore new strategies, and engage with thought leaders to stay ahead of evolving market trends.

You've Got This!

Building wealth is a marathon, not a sprint. With the knowledge you've gained, you're equipped to navigate the markets, avoid common pitfalls, and make informed decisions that align with your financial goals.

I'm incredibly proud of the progress you've made. This isn't the end—it's just the beginning of your wealth-building journey.

My favourite quote, which is the only quote included twice in my book

Become a Millionaire in One Year

Here's to your success!

CONNECT WITH LISA N EDWARDS AT

- https://lisanedwards.com/
- https://thousandtomillions.com/
- https://linktr.ee/LisaNEdwards
- https://gettingstartedincrypto.com/

Made in United States
Orlando, FL
04 November 2026

90208351R00134